NONE YARDS!

30 Years of John Madden in the Broadcast Booth

Tom Danyluk

Copyright © 2018 Tom Danyluk
All rights reserved.
ISBN: 1718950578
ISBN-13: 978-1718950573

That's one of those none-yard passes on third down. I have never understood that.... You have to find a guy that's open beyond the first-down mark. To me that's a wasted play. You should've just taken the ball and flopped on it if you're gonna do that.

—John Madden, Giants at Chiefs (9/10/95)

John Madden and Pat Summerall in their warmup before Super Bowl XVI – Bengals versus 49ers.

CONTENTS

	Preface	i
1	Coaches	1
2	Quarterbacks	8
3	Running Backs	25
4	Receivers & Tight Ends	43
5	Offensive Line	51
6	Defensive Line	60
7	The Linebackers	68
8	Defensive Backs	73
9	Special Teams	80
10	Stadiums & Officials	89
11	Strategy & Coaching	96
12	Other Stuff	105
	All-Time All-Madden Team	117
	Index	119
	Credits	124

🏈 PREFACE 🏈

I had a cousin who was a real killer on the piano. No formal lessons or training. Just Honkey-tonk, Ragtime, Gershwin and Ellington. *Name the tune, brother. Whaddaya wanna hear*? Then he'd lean over the keys and put it all together like a kiddie puzzle. *That was in C... Now, here it is in G.*

Once I asked him, "How can you do this? How does someone just sit down and teach themselves the piano?" His response didn't exactly clear up the mystery.

"Well," he answered in blunt thoughtfulness, "you gotta know where the sounds are at."

I open with this story because it essentially mirrors the way John Madden gave us pro football on television for 30 years. He knew where the sounds were at. He taught us, in that blue-collar eloquence of his, about the muscle and strategy and nuances of the National Football League. And of all the quotes I've ever read about Madden's far-reaching appeal as a broadcaster, the one from ex-CBS producer Jim Silman speared it straight to the core:

"Madden," Silman said, "has added a new dimension to broadcasting. He bridges the gap between the too-technical and the too-entertaining."

Silman offered this prescience way back in 1980, while Madden was still learning to handle a live microphone, while he was still transitioning from the rampaging, oft-hated Oakland Raiders coach to Miller Lite carnival barker to the most beloved and decorated color analyst (16 Emmys, Pro Football Hall of Fame, etc.) in TV history.

Pat Summerall was Madden's long-time setup man – 13 years with CBS then eight more at Fox Sports. In contrast to Madden, Summerall was a master of word count when it came to delivering his play-by-play. A sketch artist. A technician. Years ago, I asked him how it felt working in Madden's china shop, surrounded by all that enthusiasm and broken glass, where display tables got bumped and decorum came crashing to the floor.

"Our styles were polar opposite," Summerall answered. "Yet somehow we complemented each other perfectly. That became evident in our first few broadcasts. We had a natural rhythm. I'd take the wheel, while John looked out the window and told you what he saw."

Summerall's style came directly from working alongside Ray Scott, CBS's top play-by-play man in the '60s and early '70s. Scott's game plan each Sunday was to provide the framework – names and down and distance – then let the TV cameras show you the rest. Words should be rationed, not spilled. "Tarkenton. Gilliam. To the five." An approach that rubbed off heavily on Summerall, who became a rationist himself.

"On the other hand," Summerall said, "John's style was to basically let it fly. Whatever came into his head. He had the knowledge and understanding of a head coach, yet he was loose and colorful and eager to discuss the nuances of the game. And his enthusiasm was genuine. It was like sitting next to the world's greatest – and most knowledgeable – fan."

"There were two difficult things at first," Madden told *Sports Illustrated* in 1983. "One was not being on the field. I seemed so disassociated, disconnected from the game. The other was learning to talk about what was on the screen. I would see so many things all over the field. I'd be talking about a defensive back who had slipped down, and the picture on the monitor was the quarterback. You don't have time to premeditate. It's all reaction, and it has to be instantaneous reaction to the monitor, to what's happening on the field, to what the director is cutting to."

Madden joined CBS after retiring from the Raiders in 1979. He spent the '79 and '80 seasons tangoing around with several partners, mainly with seasoned play-by-play man Gary Bender. Bender said he immediately recognized Madden's potential as an analyst, but also understood the kind of untamed work-in-progress he was inheriting.

"I had the reputation of being kind of a coach to young announcers," Bender said, "at grooming them and bringing them along. So they moved John from Frank Glieber and assigned him to me. The network felt he had this tremendous potential and wanted to develop it. They thought I was the right fit for him.

"We started together in the 1980 preseason and, quite honestly, John struggled. At a *lot* of things. For one, he had a problem with this practice called the 'ten-second limit' – meaning, you get the replay and the analyst has to put it into a ten-second capsule then give the mic back to the play-by-play man for the next snap of the ball. The 'ten-second limit' really handcuffed him.

"Another thing John couldn't handle was people talking to him in his headset. We were in Foxborough doing a game, and they were talking into his headset while he was speaking. He got very upset and took off the headset and stormed out of the booth for a while."

Without question, Bender's early tutoring is a key factor in Madden's development. The polishing started here. So, as I'm reviewing the transcript of my chat with Bender, it seems best to just give you the whole interview, rather than weave his quotes in and out like some revolving door. He had a lot to say. The rest of it went like this:

*****

It seems that, when CBS paired Madden with you, he was still as demonstrative and emotional in the booth as he had been on the sideline, that he still hadn't learned to calm down. True?

BENDER: Oh, absolutely. He was no wallflower in that sense. There was a time in Philadelphia where he was flailing his arms around and knocked my glasses right off my face. They flew out of the press box and into the crowd! We had to send somebody from the crew into the stands to get my glasses or else I wouldn't be able to see the game.

I remember another time we were doing a Lions game in the Pontiac Silverdome. We would always open the broadcast with a quick "on-camera," where the viewers can see both of us talking and discussing the upcoming game. We started the broadcast and suddenly his headset didn't work. He got very upset and threw it over the side of the booth. A few people rushed in to help. They were crawling on the floor underneath him, looking for the problem, and it was taking some time.

Finally, they give John a hand-mic to use until the headset was fixed. I figured, okay, problem solved. But instead, as we were continuing along, he suddenly just shut down on me. He wasn't commenting at all. We'd go to a replay and he was giving barely any analysis. I was getting madder and madder at him.

We got to the commercial break and I said, "John, you gotta fight through these technical problems! I've talked to you about this before! You can't let this drag you down!" He gave me this frustrated look and said, "I know, I know, I've got to do better."

Were you...

BENDER: Hold on, there's more. The game continued on, and when we got to the next commercial John spoke up and said, "I know what the problem is. I can't *talk* with something in my hands. My hands need to be free." So, I took the hand mic from him and gave him my headset. We went back on-air and suddenly he was "John

Madden" again. He came back to life. He had to use both his hands while talking. That was the cure.

Can you recall a specific moment in those early years when it finally clicked for Madden, when he suddenly found his comfort zone as a broadcaster?

BENDER: I do, yes! It was during a preseason game in Cincinnati. For some unknown reason it suddenly clicked for him that day. He suddenly got it. His body language in the booth suddenly changed. He came out of his cocoon. It was truly an astounding thing to see.

What happened was, he got onto the topic of the jersey numbers on the uniforms – "That number doesn't fit this player…that number belongs on a different position." Jersey numbers, that was the trigger. It was the first time he'd ever talked about that. Those jerseys seemed to throw some psychological switch and he really came to life that day as a broadcaster. And he stayed there. He never regressed back.

Did you ever ask him about that broadcast? About what happened that day?

BENDER: No. In fact, I made it a point to *never* to ask him. My thought was to leave it alone. Don't mess with success. From that day on, my instincts told me to just give him room to work. I never stepped on John or tried to cut back on what he was doing. I didn't have a big ego. In return, I had the most success I ever had as a broadcaster. Simply because John was so good. He's a once-in-a-lifetime guy.

What was your relationship with Madden like outside of the booth?

BENDER: We grew close very quickly. I think the reason was because I was the first steady partner he ever had in broadcasting. He would say things like, "We're in the same foxhole," or "Gary, I really need you," meaning he needed someone to coach him. In that way, won me over instantly.

Despite his big presence and reputation, I was never intimidated by John. There are coaches that can intimidate you, but John never did. He always made me feel like we were best friends, that we were "in this together." We'd sit around and discuss things and he'd drink his Tab cola all day. He'd drink a dozen or so in one sitting, one after another.

I also knew there had to be a tougher side of John that I never got to see. To coach the Oakland Raiders you had to have *some* kind of toughness. I suppose I did see it once, at a game in Foxborough. He got upset and slammed his headset down and really chewed out our director over something. The guy was actually in tears over it. I didn't see that side of John very often, but from that incident I could tell he could be tough and very demanding.

Tell me about Madden's preparation going into a telecast. How did it differ from other analysts you had worked with?

BENDER: John *completely* changed CBS's pregame discipline for NFL football. Before he came aboard, we'd just fly in the Saturday before a game, attend a production meeting, then maybe meet with a few coaches and players. John changed that immediately. We were now going in *two* days earlier. We were now watching and studying game film and getting a much deeper education. John instituted that change. From then on, everybody started doing that in their coverage.

As the film was running in those meetings, John would be explaining things to us. Once in a while there'd be a knock at the door. It would be a coach or two from the home team wanting to talk to John. They wanted to see what John had discovered, what he actually thought about their team and the upcoming game. They reveled in his analysis. Of course, he had to be careful. He didn't want to give away any inside information from either club.

Your last broadcast together was the 1980 Wildcard between the Rams and the Cowboys. Did you know going into that game that your partnership was ending?

BENDER: I had a gut feeling, but I didn't know for sure. Our goal for 1981 was to do the Super Bowl together. But later that spring the story came out that they were going to have John work with Pat Summerall and Vin Scully. John actually came to me and said, "Gary, I really want to keep working with you." We went to the president of CBS to plead our case. I knew it was futile, but John did that for me and I really appreciated it. After that meeting we knew there was no chance. He was leaving me.

In '81 John did games with both Vin and Pat. Vin's discipline was baseball, and he was truly the wordmeister. He commanded the mic. That was his domain. He wasn't necessarily looking to share the microphone. The story goes that while he was teamed with Jim Brown and George Allen, Vin actually went to the network heads and asked if he could start doing games by *himself* – with no analysts in the booth. Of course, they shot that down.

After the test run was over, they realized that Summerall was a much better fit for John, mainly because Scully wasn't willing to give John enough room to work. Summerall gave him *lots* of room. As a broadcaster, Summerall didn't give you a whole lot of insight, but he brilliantly knew how to lead Madden into a topic. From there, John would just amplify it.

*****

Question to the TV audience: What was it about Madden's style that made him so undeniably popular, "a sensation overnight," as Bender called him? Can anyone quantify it, put a true frame around it? As a coach, Madden was a ranter and a raver on the sideline, the Oakland wild man, yet he was surprisingly calm and demur when dealing with the press. A contradiction.

What changed when he finally put on that headset? And why was his message and style so fully embraced by the entire spectrum of NFL viewers?

It wasn't just his football knowledge; many top coaches have sat in the analyst's chair and were nothing special when they opened their mouths. Madden never tried to dazzle you with playbook talk, anyway. In fact, he avoided that kind of complexity.

It wasn't just those cartoonish *WHAPs* and *BAMs* that he'd throw on top of a replay. That was gimmick stuff, and gimmicks wear thin. And yet, even over decades, viewers never tired of it.

He wasn't a comedian or jokester. Or a storyteller, a tales-around-the-campfire guy. You'd get the occasional "I remember" from his Raider days, but he never leaned too heavily on the nostalgia crutch.

Then what was his appeal? Can anyone put it into words? Why was John Madden so damn good every damn Sunday, even in the washout games? I mean, WHAT WAS IT?

"I have a theory on that," says former defensive tackle Pat Toomay, who played under Madden for two seasons. "I watched John coach and I've listened to him as a broadcaster, and there's definitely a common element as to why he was successful at both.

"I say Madden's trick was having the ability to communicate the simple *thrill* of being in one's body, if that makes any sense. To put the raw physicality of football into words. The grunting and banging…the rolling in the muck and crap…the 'earthly entanglements' of line play.

"Football is violence. But he could slip under the violence aspect, under that storm, and relate the game's soul to the audience. *Those are human beings in those uniforms. This is what they're feeling. This is what they're going through.*

"It all comes from the fact that John has always revered football. Not loved it. *Revered* it. Everything about the game. The memories of old days, the anticipation of training camp, highs and lows, the joy of just playing. All of that remains at the front of his mind, like an open book. It's always there. He never puts it away."

Bob Stenner, who produced NFL football for years with both CBS and Fox, has his own theory on the core of Madden's appeal.

"I feel what truly elevated Madden as an announcer was his natural curiosity about people," Stenner once told me. "He was always asking questions, not just to coaches or players but to everyone. He wanted to *know* things. It was genuine interest.

"Along with that, John was a natural teacher. As the game was unfolding, he'd explain things and point out the details. He had the patience for that.

"Now you have his big personality who loved gathering facts and stories about the game, and who loved educating his audience. That combination translated extremely well into broadcasting."

However, there is an addendum to all this theory that can't be overstated – the overwhelming influence of Pat Summerall. It's highly likely that, without Summerall as conductor, Madden would never have reached the superstar heights as a broadcaster.

Want proof? Go back and watch Madden's pre-Summerall work, his days with Bender and Scully and Glieber. He was hardly a polished performer. His content wasn't nearly as striking or vibrant – or confident. At times he was timid and dull. Even boring.

By the end of the 1980 season – his last before Summerall – Madden still had that god-awful habit of regurgitating what everyone could see already on the replay. *You see, he made a cut here and picked up a block here and was able to pick up a few more yards,* etc.

That all changed when Summerall stepped in. Suddenly Madden launched into full *Ka-Boom*. His energy level went sky-high. The depth of his analysis became richer. His playfulness with the camera shots increased. The "Miller Lite" character joined the show. This was no longer some ex-coach with a microphone. This was now *John Madden, Number-One NFL Analyst*.

And Summerall was the catalyst.

"From the standpoint of television presentation," NBC's Charlie Jones once told me, "Summerall is the greatest play-by-play broadcaster ever. No question, *he* made Madden great. He did it by steering him, by setting him up, allowing him time, not letting his own ego get involved.

"There's an old story that goes back to the heyday of radio. When you're conducting an interview, you are the supporting actor. The person you are interviewing is the star. Your job is to make *him* the star. If that works, you both win. That's very difficult for some announcers to do, especially the younger ones. Summerall did it purely by nature."

"What made that pair so dynamic," said Stenner, "was that John could be longwinded and full of enthusiasm, while Pat was always so succinct. I use the airplane analogy with them. John flew the plane anywhere he wanted to go, to whatever height and direction his curiosity took him, and Pat would still land it safely. That's a good feeling to have in the booth. There was nothing John could say that Pat couldn't fix or clean up. Summerall was a genius that way.

"With some broadcast teams, if the game goes south then the whole broadcast goes south. Not with those two. They had a gift of being able to raise their level of performance in blowout games. Anything we'd show them [on camera], they'd make it interesting. It could be pigeons. It could be the sunset or the moon. Sometimes we'd put these random shots on the air, irrelevant things, just to have fun and see what they'd say."

What also cannot be overstated here is the fact that Summerall himself was a former NFL player – ten seasons with the Cardinals, Giants and Lions. Most play-by-play men are not. Glieber, Bender and Scully certainly weren't. They were the graduate types, classically preened for the job. Summerall came to CBS straight from the locker room. He'd been through the kinds of battles Madden was talking about. He knew the smells of training camp, and the sound an injury makes when it's a bad one. It was *that* deep-seated connection which allowed their broadcasts to shine.

"There is no play-by-play guy that knows the game as well as Pat," Madden told *The Washington Post* in 1985. "He not only played the game, he was once a coach under Harlan Svare with the Rams."

The significance of this reminds me of another story. This one is about a friend who found his way into a Battle of the Bulge reunion being held at some Baltimore hotel. My friend, of course, was never in the Bulge or anywhere near it. Just a curious observer who stopped on by – uninvited.

"I love World War II history," my friend said, "so I found their conference room. All these old soldiers with medals, talking, telling stories. A few were laughing. It didn't seem too serious. So, I walked around and eavesdropped for a while. I had all these questions I wanted to ask…about the weather, the Germans, their tanks.

"Finally, I picked out a guy with a friendly face and struck up a conversation. He asked if I was a reporter for *The Washington Times*. I said, 'No, but I'm a historian about the war.' He walked away. I tried talking to two or three other guys and got the same brush-off.

"I knew to bolt from the Battle of the Bulge reunion. The message was clear: No Outsiders. No Guests. If you weren't one of them, they wouldn't talk. They weren't sharing stories with anyone."

In John Madden's world, Summerall was no reunion crasher. He was "one of them." He also understood violent hits and aching knees and booting a ball on frozen days. Together, as a duo, the pressure was surely off. No need to lean on their own war stories. They could relax and open up and peel the layers off someone else's battles. Like the old war advice from Hemingway:

"Don't go back to visit the old front. If you have pictures in your head of something that happened in the night in the mud at Paschendaele or the first wave working up the slope of Vimy, do not try and go back to verify them. It is no good.... Go to someone else's front if you want to. There your imagination will help you out and you may be able to picture the things that happened.

What I present in *None Yards!* is a verbal history, a collection of words from John Madden's TV broadcasts. Live, from someone else's front. His thoughts on coaches and officials and weather, on Joe Montana and Lawrence Taylor and Reggie White. His opinions on clods with painted faces and the evil of artificial turf and "throwing for none yards" when you need seven.

It's truly All-Madden. Pro football as he saw it. But after queueing up 300+ games on the disc player, my ears are sore. I hear him in my sleep. He bumps the glasses off my nightstand. Time to get it out in print.

Tom Danyluk
Oak Park, IL
May 2018

Chapter 1: COACHES

Coach Tom Landry in command of the Dallas Cowboys sideline.

On former USC and Tampa Bay Bucs coach John McKay: He's a fine man. I've known John for 25 years. As a matter of fact, I went to the University of Oregon for one year and John McKay was my coach. –*Packers at Buccaneers (10/21/79)*

On the optimal head-coaching arrangement: I've always felt that the quality of a coaching job in the NFL is directly related to how many people you have over you. The Utopian job would be to have your own club and be your own coach – like Paul Brown and George Halas. If they were going to have a meeting, they had it with themselves. The next best thing would be to have one person over you. That's why I felt the Oakland job was one of the best. –*Inside Sports (August 1980)*

On not wearing a headset while coaching the Raiders: I probably wasn't smart enough to talk and listen at the same time. –*Giants at 49ers (11/23/80)*

On Eagles coach Dick Vermeil sleeping three nights a week at the stadium: I *understand* that. But you don't *do* that over a long period of time. –*Giants at Eagles (11/22/81)*

On, once upon a time, firing Redskins coach Joe Gibbs: He and I were at San Diego State together and we would argue all the time. One time we had an argument where I said, "If you do that, you will *never* coach again on defense." He did it, so he never coached again on defense. Don Coryell made him an offensive coach; that's how he got where he is today. It was a ridiculous argument. He was coaching the alumni and I was coaching against the alumni. I asked him, "Tell me the plays you're gonna run so we can work against them." He said, "No!" I said, "Either tell me the plays, or you won't coach defense anymore." He didn't tell me the plays. *–Redskins at Giants (11/21/82)*

On the rumor of best friend John Robinson leaving USC for the NFL: I don't think so, especially if he stays in football in some capacity. I don't think he'll ever go into pro football. *–Giants at Lions (11/25/82)*
NOTE: On February 14, 1983, Robinson was named head coach of the Los Angeles Rams.

On Dallas coach Tom Landry not being easily rattled: We were talking about Tony Dorsett on Saturday, whether he'd be able to play or not. Tom Landry said, "I don't know. I'll talk to him tomorrow about it." I would've been a basket case, a nervous wreck, if I didn't know if my best player was going to play or not the day before the game. *–Eagles at Cowboys (12/26/82)*

On the future of burned-out Eagles coach Dick Vermeil: I wouldn't be surprised if this was his last coaching game in the NFL, and by his own choice. I have no reason. I just have a feeling that Dick Vermeil may not be coaching next year, and I don't think he's going any place else...Sometimes you just burn out. There's no more there. *–Giants at Eagles (1/2/83)*
NOTE: Vermeil retired from coaching on January 10, 1983.

On coaches using written notes on the sideline: I've always said that by the time you get to the game, if you have to write it down to remember it, you shouldn't use it anyway. *–Rams at Giants (9/4/83)*

On first-year Giants coach Bill Parcells: He really is an open and honest guy. I think, if he has time, someday he's going to be one of the real good head coaches in this league. *–Giants at Cowboys (9/18/83)*
NOTE: In 2013, Parcells was inducted into the Pro Football Hall of Fame.

On Cowboys coach Tom Landry, in a suit, stopping a player who ran out of bounds: I've been watching baseball, that World Series, and managers always wear those baseball uniforms. Heck, they don't *play*. I was thinking, what would happen if they said, "Hey, that's a good rule. Football coaches should do that!" Can you see Tom Landry in a uniform? He'd probably be number 19. [Asst. coach] Mike Ditka, he'd tape up. [Asst. coach]

Eric Gamble would be 78, shirt tail hanging out. Football coaches in football uniforms. –*Eagles at Cowboys (10/16/83)*

On whether Giants should retain head coach Bill Parcells after a 3-12-1 season: I think he deserves to be back. This has been a tough year. Anything bad that can happen happened here. I think if you're gonna hire a coach, you have to give him a chance. This year he really didn't have a chance. He's a good guy, and I hope that he is back… Had the Steelers gotten rid of Chuck Noll when he was 1-13 his first year, I don't think they would've won four Super Bowls. –*Giants at Redskins (12/17/83)*

On Rams coach John Robinson being a heavy underdog at Washington: John Robinson said, "If we could set it up somehow where our offense couldn't even see the scoreboard, I'd like to do that. I don't want them to feel that they have to panic, that they have to force things, that they have to make stupid mistakes. Just play." –*NFC Playoffs, Rams at Redskins (1/1/84)*

On coaches using the word "twinge" to describe an injury: That's a coach's word for *You hope he's not bad. He has a little knee…a little ankle.* That means you hope he can play next week. –*NFC Championship Game, 49ers at Redskins (1/8/84)*

On an overzealous Raiders assistant coach: I used to have a coach who would stand on the sideline and tell the guys before the play, "Watch out for the screen! Watch out for the draw! Watch out for the pass! Watch out for the run! Watch out for the quarterback draw! Watch out for this!" Then, whatever [the offense] did, he'd say, "I told you so!" –*Cowboys at Chargers (8/17/85)*

On the Raiders' 0-2 start to the 1986 season: [Coach] Tom Flores said yesterday, "I thought about that Denver game and we played well *offensively*. In the Redskin game we played well *defensively*. Then on Friday night I had all my papers out and I was worrying. Then I started thinking *We really aren't bad*. So, I took all my papers, threw them in a bag and watched a movie with my wife." Sometimes you do that as a coach. You have these little meetings with yourself. –*Giants at Raiders (9/21/86)*

On former Jets coach Weeb Ewbank: I remember years ago we were playing the Jets at Shea Stadium. Weeb Ewbank, before the game, told me, "Johnny" – I knew then to watch out when he said *Johnny* – "Look up there into the second deck; there's that little flag. That's how you tell how the wind is going here." The whole game I was scared to death to look up at that flag because I knew that wasn't true. I'd catch myself looking up and I'd look back down because I knew he had a fan or something up there. –*Cowboys at Giants (11/2/86)*

On Bears coach Mike Ditka: Now *there* is a coach. We were talking to his wife Diane last night and she was saying, "He doesn't know anything. He can't fix anything or do anything." One time she called home and he was fixing an electrical outlet, so he had all the electricity turned off. He picked up the phone and said, "I'm working on the lights here. How'd ya get ahold of me? I've got the electricity turned off." He thought if you shut all the electricity off, the phone can't ring. That's my kinda guy. He's a coach! He doesn't know these Alexander Graham Bell deals. –*Bears at Cowboys (12/21/86)*

On stress eating: It's a funny thing how Joe Gibbs was walking around on Friday eating everything in sight. Coaches that gain weight will tend to gain weight during the season. When you get nervous you tend to eat all the time. Joe Gibbs is one of those guys. I think Buddy Ryan has a little of that in him, too. I gained weight. I would work long, hard hours, not much sleep. You'd think you'd lose weight. You *gain* weight because of how many hours you're awake. You have a lot of meals in that time. If you're only awake 12 hours, you get three meals; if you're awake 18 you get one or two more meals in there. –*Eagles at Redskins (9/13/87)*

On Giants coach Bill Parcells' sad demeanor as his '87 strike team loses again: Bill Parcells has to be going [through] the whole spectrum. In this same year of 1987, he remembers being carried off the field in the Super Bowl at the Rose Bowl in Pasadena – to this. He's probably going to be 0-4 at the end of the day. It's the height and the depth. –*Redskins at Giants (10/11/87)*

On Eagles head coach Buddy Ryan's myriad of defenses: The one thing the Eagles do more than any other team in the NFL is change their defenses. Buddy Ryan was saying they use 20 different coverages and 10 different fronts. "The bad news," he says, "is we only play about two of them right." –*Eagles at Jets (12/20/87)*

On playing the same team during the preseason and regular season: Buddy Ryan said he learned this from Weeb Ewbank. Ewbank said, "If you ever play someone in the preseason then play them again in the regular season, *lose* to them in the preseason. An old Weeb Ewbank trick. –*Eagles at Jets (12/20/87)*

On disheveled Vikings head coach Jerry Burns: He looks like he's been through *three or four* games…and a car wash. –*NFC Wildcard, Vikings at Saints (1/3/88)*

On 49ers coach Bill Walsh retirement rumors: There's a lot of speculation as to whether Bill Walsh will be back to coach the 49ers again. I don't think he will. I think the end is near, and I think it's gonna be his choice. Not [owner] Eddie DiBartolo's choice, but Bill Walsh's choice. Eddie DiBartolo said he would like to have him back, but I don't know if Bill Walsh is going to be back. –*NFC Playoffs, Vikings at 49ers (1/1/89)*

NOTE: This would prove to be Walsh's last home game as 49ers head coach.

On 49ers coach Bill Walsh winning his third NFC title: I wouldn't be surprised if Bill Walsh takes the 49ers to the Super Bowl then gets his hat, goes off into the sunset, does something else. I think that Bill Walsh is one of the great coaches in the NFL, of all time, and this will be his third Super Bowl. And I think he's at an age – 57 years old – where he's at the end. –*NFC Championship Game, 49ers at Bears (1/8/89)*

NOTE: After winning Super Bowl XXIII, Walsh retired from coaching on January 26, 1989.

On Cowboys' first-year head coach Jimmy Johnson: The other day Rickey Jackson, the linebacker for the Saints, was saying, "I don't know what's gonna happen at halftime, but I'll guarantee if we're ahead, Jimmy Johnson is gonna be in there throwing everything, including blackboards." Jimmy Johnson was an assistant at Pittsburgh when Rickey Jackson played there. He said, "I'll guarantee you, he's gonna throw blackboards. He might even throw some of the guys out of the locker room and into the parking lot." –*Cowboys at Saints (9/10/89)*

On former Miami Hurricanes head coach Jimmy Johnson: Yesterday we were talking to him in his [hotel] room. The Miami-Wisconsin game was on and it was 34-to-3. He said, "Just think, if I weren't here, I'd be there. And they'd be saying Jimmy Johnson's piling it on again." –*Cowboys at Saints (9/10/89)*

On Eagles head coach Buddy Ryan: In the preseason, [QB] Randall Cunningham wanted to go see Whitney Houston. It was a Saturday-night game. So, he played the first half and Buddy Ryan let he and [TE] Keith Jackson leave in the second half. When people say that Buddy Ryan is a player's coach, it's *that* type of thing that makes him a player's coach. I don't know if I would ever do that. –*Eagles at Cowboys (11/23/89)*

On Cowboys coach Jimmy Johnson upsetting the undefeated Redskins: Of all the games that I've watched and that we've done together, I think that Jimmy Johnson has done more with less than any game I can remember. I think this is one of the best coaching jobs that I have ever seen. –*Cowboys at Redskins (11/24/91)*

On discipline: I'll tell you one thing about coaching. It's a lot easier to start off tough and lighten up than it is to lighten up then try and turn tough. – *Packers at Vikings (12/21/91)*

On Eagles defensive coordinator Bud Carson: He'll keep mixing those defenses up and mixing them up, and if he finds something you can't block, he'll give it to you all day. *–Redskins at Eagles (9/19/93)*

On Vince Lombardi: Vince Lombardi was my idol. I wanted to be just like Vince Lombardi. He was the greatest pro football coach ever. I remember when I was a young coach I thought I knew it all. I could talk about any play for fifteen minutes and I thought, "I know football. I know plays," etc. So, I went to a clinic in Reno, Nevada in 1963 or 1964, and Vince Lombardi spoke on one play – the Green Bay sweep – for eight hours. After listening to Vince Lombardi, I had more respect for him than any man I had ever known. And I said to myself, "You don't know football." *–Giants at Packers (9/17/95)*

On Packers coach Mike Holmgren's relationship with 49ers QB Steve Young: Mike Holmgren was Steve Young's quarterback coach at BYU. In the first game that he was the quarterback coach and Steve Young was the starter, Young threw six interceptions against Georgia. And Mike Holmgren told him, "You're gonna get benched, and I'm gonna get fired." *–49ers at Packers (11/1/98)*

On Saints coach Mike Ditka's aggressive gum chewing: I would hate to be that gum. How'd you like to be the gum on the shelf and you see Mike Ditka coming down to buy you? He kills that gum. He whacks it. He snaps it. It doesn't have a chance. He doesn't let it breathe at all. *–Saints at Dolphins (11/29/98)*

On Rams coach Dick Vermeil: When I first started coaching, we used to go to coaching clinics, and coaches from the big colleges would give talks and we'd all take notes. Big ol' linemen like me would always take sloppy notes. We'd put them in our back pocket. You sweat on them, you spill something on them, you lose them. Dick Vermeil took the *neatest* notes. Then you know what he would do? If you would leave your address with him, he'd send you a copy of his notes. For nothing. And he did it for every coach in the state of California. He was that kinda guy. *–NFC Playoffs, Vikings at Rams (1/16/00)*

On Dave Campo's disastrous first game as Cowboys head coach: Dave Campo, all his life, has been dreaming of being a head coach. Thirty years in coaching and this is his first head coaching job, his first game, his first half. And in his dreams, he wasn't losing 24-to-3. *–Eagles at Cowboys (9/3/00)*

On a penalty-filled night by the Patriots: As a coach, turnovers always kinda reflect your discipline. If you have a lot of penalties, it always goes right to you, that you don't have a disciplined team. That's one of the things that always eats on a coach. I know Bill Belichick very well, and penalties mean sloppy play and a lot of stupid mistakes. And you don't want to be the coach of that type of team. *–Patriots at Broncos (11/3/03)*

NOTE: Over his decade as Raiders head coach, Madden's teams ranked in the top ten in penalties eight times.

Chapter 2: QUARTERBACKS

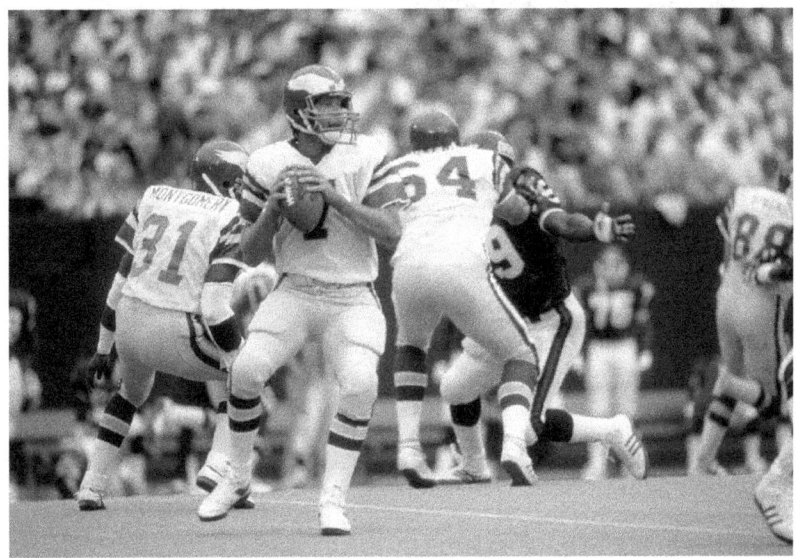

Eagles QB Ron Jaworski fires into the N.Y. Giants defense.

On coaching against Saints QB Archie Manning: I remember we went down to New Orleans. We were a fine team at that time and we got into a game with them and Archie was running all over the field. He was scrambling. He was holding the ball. They had option plays and everything. As we were going off at halftime I said to him, "You know, you really shouldn't run that much. This is the National Football League. You're not supposed to do that." He didn't listen at all. He kept it up. –*Saints at 49ers, Madden's first CBS telecast (9/23/79)*

On QBs calling their own plays: I always had my quarterback call his own plays. I like the play to come from *within* the huddle. There's a difference when you have the players out there on the other side of the stripes, the guys that are playing, doing it. I always liked the play to come from within *that* group, where it was theirs. –*Saints at 49ers (9/23/79)*

On immobile Broncos QB Craig Morton: When teams play against Craig Morton, they usually dust off their blitzes. –*Saints at Broncos (11/4/79)*

On competition at the QB position: I always felt you had to have a number-one guy. He's *it*. And the guy behind him should be unhappy. Because if you ever have a situation where you have a No. 1 and the quarterback behind him is satisfied or happy that he's No. 2, then when you need him he's not ready to play. I thought that when the second guy was complaining about not playing, wanting to be traded, it was a very healthy thing. That's *not* a negative thing. *–Packers at Rams (9/21/80)*

On Eagles QB Ron Jaworski completing a long, third-down pass: Ron Jaworski really showed us something there. Anyone can pass on the first down, on second down. But when you're third down and you need 18 yards, that takes a special type of thing. That's where the real quarterbacks shine, in those situations. *–Eagles at Seahawks (11/8/80)*

On Giants QB Phil Simms taking a beating: [Coach] Ray Perkins said Phil Simms was tough, but you don't want to prove it on every down. *–Giants at 49ers (11/23/80)*

On the downside of emotion: A quarterback can't get too emotional because it shows in his touch. *–Falcons at Eagles (12/7/80)*

On running quarterbacks: We always talk about these *running* quarterbacks. They really don't have to be able to run. All they have to be able to do is take a few steps right or left…a few quick steps, get out of the way, square their shoulders up and find something else [downfield]. *–NFC Wildcard, Rams at Cowboys (12/28/80)*

On Eagles QB Ron Jaworski bitching at an official: That's why they call him "Jaws." *–Eagles at Giants (9/6/81)*

On coolness of Browns QB Brian Sipe: MADDEN: Look at Sipe. You talk about people that are unflappable, *there* is an unflappable man. I like that word. He's truly unflappable. There's nothing that can flap him.

VIN SCULLY: You usually don't see flappable quarterbacks, anyway.

MADDEN: Jaworski's kinda flappable! Norm Van Brocklin was a flappable one! *–Falcons at Browns (9/27/81)*

On jittery quarterbacks: You can't always tell when a quarterback is nervous…by what he says or how his eyes look. But the one thing that's a giveaway is the feet. When a quarterback is nervous, his feet are always moving, and that's where the nervousness comes out. *–Giants at Eagles (11/22/81)*

On an unconventional delivery by Giants QB Scott Brunner: On that last play – where he took the ball and his feet were both pointing straight ahead and he threw it out to the right, just flicked it out there – that's one of the things Ray Perkins says he likes about Scott Brunner. He says he doesn't always have to be in perfect position to throw the ball. That's true of all great quarterbacks. They don't always have to get that perfect thing. They can throw it from a lot of angles. –*Giants at Eagles (11/22/81)*

After a low pass thrown by Oilers QB Kenny Stabler: When he used to play for Oakland and did that, he'd come to the sideline and say, "Highball drinker, lowball thrower." –*Falcons at Oilers (11/29/81)*

On football's toughest position: The toughest position in football is being the parent of a quarterback. –*Raiders at 49ers (8/14/82)*

On Raiders QB Jim Plunkett's ability to throw under pressure: Jim Plunkett is amazing. He can throw the ball under heavy fire. It's a stunt... [Rams DE Jack] Youngblood was right there, yet somehow he got that ball through to Todd Christensen. The darndest positions. Watch the pressure... He's spinning, turning, whirling, getting hit in the back, folded, knocked down, doing flips, rolls, cartwheels. All in a day's work. –*Rams at Raiders (12/18/82)*

On the definition of "quick release": That's what a quick release is: the time the eyes see a guy open and decide on who they're going to throw to until the ball leaves the hand. That thing, that mechanism between the eyes and the hand. –*NFC Championship Game, Cowboys at Redskins (1/22/83)*

On Cowboys backup QB Gary Hogeboom: It's really tough for a backup quarterback to come in a regular game. Then you make it a *playoff* game and that would be tougher. You make it a *championship* game and that would be one of the most difficult things they have to do – especially when you're behind, 14-3. If the Cowboys were ahead, they could go to a lot of that running game and ball control. But Hogeboom has to come in and score points. –*NFC Championship Game, Cowboys at Redskins (1/22/83)*

On Falcons QB Steve Bartkowski: The interesting thing – and I really don't understand it – is that Steve Bartkowski is the number-one rated quarterback in the NFL, but the Atlanta Falcons are ranked *tenth* in pass offense. And Bartkowski's been the quarterback the whole time! There's something wrong there. That's one of those things where everything's going good but *not* good. –*Falcons at Jets (10/23/83)*

On comparing cocky Redskins QB Joe Theismann to erratic Jets QB Richard Todd: Before [coach] Joe Walton came to the New York Jets, he was the offensive coordinator of the Washington Redskins. We were talking to him yesterday about the difference between Todd and Theismann. He said, "They're *totally* different. Theismann had *too much* confidence. You had to kinda tone him down. Richard Todd really doesn't *have* that confidence; you have to build up him all the time. They're two totally different personalities." –*Falcons at Jets (10/23/83)*

On the pass rush: One thing a quarterback can't do is anticipate a rush. A rush is either there or it's not. But you can't *believe* it's there. –*Cowboys at Giants (10/30/83)*

On why only certain teams are successful using screen plays: I think a lot of it has to do with the quarterback. I remember [49ers] John Brodie was great at that. You hold the ball...you fight that line...you get the linebackers back and just drop it in there. –*Cowboys at Giants (10/30/83)*

On Cowboys QB Danny White: Danny White has those eyes, that look of intensity, doesn't he? He always looks like he's going hunting or something. Big game hunting. Look at him – he calls that play and he's looking right at those linemen and they don't miss a thing. *You gotta get that snap count, men!* –*Cardinals at Cowboys (11/24/83)*

On the naked bootleg play: I could never get my quarterback to buy that one. I'd say, "Look, if we send 'em all that way, all the [defenders] will *run* that way. Then you run the *other* way." Stabler would say, "Well, what if they don't?" –*Cardinals at Cowboys (11/24/83)*

On Redskins coach Joe Gibbs not playing backup Bob Holly during a blowout: I think Holly wants to go in, but I don't think Joe Gibbs wants to put him in. He says that he doesn't believe in that, having another quarterback come in and finish out a game. He said all they do is do sloppy things and get in bad habits. It looks like Holly was up there begging but Gibbs didn't pay any attention to him. He's just staring straight ahead. *Hey Joe, you're ahead 51-7! You don't have to stare!* You have to like that Holly, though. He won't take no for an answer. He keeps warming up. –*NFC Playoffs, Rams at Redskins (1/1/84)*

On Falcons QB Steve Bartkowski's recent illness: Talking about Steve Bartkowski being sick and missing practice on Saturday and so on. I've seen a lot of quarterbacks have great days after being sick. You don't have a lot of time for anxiety. You're worrying more about getting well than you are about the other team, and sometimes that's not a bad deal. –*Falcons at Rams (10/7/84)*
NOTE: Bartkowski completed 14 of 19 passes for 3TDs in the Falcons' win.

On QB Kenny Stabler's confidence in Super Bowl XI: We had to settle for a field goal and I was really upset. I said, "Doggonit, offense, you have to *do* this! You have to score when you get down there! We've got to *do* this!" I'm going crazy and Stabler comes up and pats me on the back and says, "Don't worry, coach, there's plenty more where that one came from." –*Packers at Lions (11/22/84)*

On the sideline crowd around 49ers QB Joe Montana: Wide receivers and tight ends always want to stay close to the quarterback. I mean, there's Russ Francis... [Dwight] Clark's talking to him...Freddie Solomon...Renaldo Nehemiah. And when the quarterback tries to get away, he goes by the kicker. Because *no one* stands around the kicker. If you want to be alone, you go next to the kicker. –*NFC Championship Game, Bears at 49ers (1/6/85)*

On erratic Buccaneers QB Steve DeBerg: DeBerg seems to be a streak quarterback. When he gets something going, it looks like you can't stop him. But the gap between "getting something going" is just too wide. –*Buccaneers at Giants (11/3/85)*

On rugged Bears QB Jim McMahon scrambling out of bounds on the opponent's sideline: McMahon is probably over on the sidelines making excuses or apologizing to the Jet guys for running out of bounds. But that's one of the things that he and Mike Ditka talked about. Ditka says, "I like you, but I like you healthy. You can't do those stupid things like throwing your body around and diving and stuff. Run out of bounds! Take the knee once in a while! You don't have to be the macho guy all the time." –*Bears at Jets (12/14/85)*

On the Cowboys offense employing the "hot receiver" concept: Gary Hogeboom is having a good day leading these Cowboys, but he's gonna have a sore day tomorrow if they keep letting one of those linebackers get free all the time. I never believed in that. They call that the "hot receiver." You let a linebacker go and the quarterback has to rid of it before he gets there. That's easy to draw up and hard to do if you're the quarterback. –*Cowboys at 49ers (12/22/85)*

On the eccentricity of Bears QB Jim McMahon: I always liked that type of quarterback. I don't think you can have a quarterback who's a normal guy. It's not a normal position; they don't do normal things. I don't think there's many great ones that *have* been normal. Roger Staubach's the closest, but even he had a few quirks. –*NFC Playoffs, Giants at Bears (1/5/86)*

On a late hit on Bears QB Jim McMahon: They have to protect quarterbacks in this league, I don't care what they say. I'm talking about *any* quarterback. You can't hit 'em after they throw it! And they let it go on and on, and you've got guys down all over the league. –*Bears at Bengals (9/28/86)*

On the value of Bears QB Jim McMahon: He throws three touchdown passes and he scores on a quarterback sneak, but other things help an offense. Sometimes just having the guy there, and the way he handles the huddle. The way he calls the play. The way he does the cadence. Sometimes these things give an offense a big lift. That was one of Kenny Stabler's greatest things – handling that huddle, being the boss, the field general. – *Bears at Bengals (9/28/86)*

On an off-balance, 50-yard completion by Broncos QB John Elway: That's not even a *great* quarterback throw, Pat. That's a Superman throw! I don't know if there's anyone else in the NFL that makes this throw. Mark Jackson runs an out then an up. But Elway, scrambling around, running, hits that thing on the run...Look at how he threw that ball, 50 yards, and hit him on the run! That is an amazing football play! –*Cowboys at Broncos (10/5/86)*

On quarterbacks throwing high over the middle, exposing their receivers: Those are the ones you go back and have a talk with the quarterback about. Of course, he's saying, "I was getting rushed; I gotta get rid of the ball!" Then he goes to the offensive linemen, and the poor offensive linemen have no one to complain to. So, they point to the center and say, "It's the snap count. *He* snapped it early!" –*Saints at Jets (10/26/86)*

On Falcons QB David Archer's 2-for-15, 2INT day against the Bears in 1985: I think that was the worst day I've ever seen by an NFL quarterback. –*Bears at Falcons (11/16/86)*

On Redskins QB Jay Schroeder: He's a guy that left college and played professional baseball and found out maybe that throwing a deep pass is easier than hitting a curve ball...I wonder if you can test that [theory]. Just standing up there and a guy throwing a hundred mile an hour fastball at you, or standing back there in the pocket with 290-pound, 4.5 guys coming at you. Which is more dangerous? Probably all in the eyes of the beholder. –*Cowboys at Redskins (11/23/86)*

On a replay of a late hit on Packers QB Randy Wright: I've always said, they protect the kickers. Watch – the ball's gone! Now, *BOOM! BOOM!* You can't do that to a *kicker*. Why do they let them do it to the quarterback? That's where they get hurt. –*Packers at Lions (11/27/86)*

On the huge list of injured QBs during the 1986 season: We've lost so many quarterbacks in the National Football League...There's still too [many late hits] going on. I have an answer. You give the referee a horn. It's not like a whistle; it doesn't stop the play. When the quarterback throws the ball, he blows the horn. Once you hear *Honk!* you can't hit the guy anymore, just like a kicker. If he doesn't go *Honk!* then you can hit him...The NFL is a passing league and it's a league of quarterbacks. You have to have a quarterback. I don't think we can just throw these guys around like that and knock them into the artificial turf, knock 'em out...I think something has to be done about it. And I don't want to hear "Put skirts on them." That's a dumb thing. That's old. *–Packers at Lions (11/27/86)*

On QB arm strength: Where you can tell the strength of a quarterback's arm is throwing the out [pattern]. *–Redskins at Broncos (12/13/86)*

On 49ers QB Joe Montana: The average quarterback throws the ball in about three seconds – *one-thousand-one, one-thousand-two, one-thousand-three*. Joe Montana will release the ball in about half that. You just can't get to him. Lawrence Taylor was saying, "It's so frustrating. I don't think I've ever had a good hit on him. For a hyper guy like me, he's the toughest guy to play against." *–NFC Playoffs, 49ers at Giants (1/4/87)*

On Redskins QB Jay Schroeder: Jay Schroeder has a strong arm. He can throw into the wind. He said, "I can throw right *through* the wind. The only thing I have to remember is keep the nose of the football down." I guess that's something like airplanes. If you put the nose up, you take off; you keep the nose down and you land. *–NFC Championship Game, Redskins at Giants (1/11/87)*

On Steelers QB Mark Malone being "much-maligned": He's had a tough time. Last year when [RB Walter] Abercrombie was out and before they got [RB] Ernest Jackson, they didn't have a running game. And they're a running team! John Stallworth was hurt and Louis Lipps was hurt...Everyone was hurt and he was playing with half a deck. Then they blamed him. He didn't have a full deck. You gotta give the man a deck! *–Giants at Steelers (9/5/87)*

On Giants replacement QB Mike Busch playing better after being knocked around: Mike Busch made a pretty good throw on that one. Sometimes you hit a quarterback and you knock some cobwebs out and you wake him up and he starts throwing pretty well. That's what Busch is doing now. I remember Kenny Stabler was that way. Sometimes he wouldn't be having a good game until someone would level him. Then he'd come up and complete ten in a row. *–Redskins at Giants (10/11/87)*

On Saints replacement QB John Fourcade: He's one of those guys that has a linebacker mentality. In fact, he was saying, "I kinda like this stuff. We come in and play in football, and if the NBA has a strike we'll go play basketball. Hockey, we'll go knock a puck around. Whoever goes on strike, we'll go play in that league." I think he's that type of guy who would. I think he'd go play hockey and be a goalie. *–Saints at Bears (10/18/87)*

On Bears replacement QB Sean Payton entering the game: I wonder if something happened to [starter] Steve Bradley. Because Mike Ditka told us yesterday, "I don't think you'll see Sean Payton. He fouled the plays up. Last week we put Payton in there and we gave him a play – first down, a running play – and he ends up in a shotgun and calls something. I don't think he's ready for this." *–Saints at Bears (10/18/87)*

On Saints replacement QB John Fourcade: Coming out of college, they thought that he was too cocky. I remember saying that I think that's good! I think cocky for a quarterback is good. You think back to the quarterbacks like Bobby Lane and Norm Van Brocklin and Joe Namath, Kenny Stabler. All those guys had that cocky thing. I'm not saying John Fourcade is in that class, but I don't think that cocky is negative in a quarterback. *–Saints at Bears (10/18/87)*

On journeyman QB Steve DeBerg: He's a guy that's not really a respected quarterback or gets as much respect as he should get. He said, "All you gotta do, if you want a great quarterback, is get me because you'll get one after that." He was at San Francisco and here comes Joe Montana. Then he goes to Denver, and here comes John Elway. Then he comes to Tampa, and here comes Steve Young and Vinnie Testaverde. *–Bears at Buccaneers (10/25/87)*

More on DeBerg: He is quite an athlete. He was a pole vaulter in high school, and they say he's a great tennis player. In fact, when he plays tennis they call him "DeBorg." They could call him "DeNicklaus" in golf. Or if he wrestles they can call him "DeHulk." Just put "De" in front of it and that's what he is. *–Bears at Buccaneers (10/25/87)*

On 49ers QB Joe Montana: One thing Joe Montana is a master at: If you're gonna give him a rush, he'll get the ball away quicker than you can rush to get him. *–49ers at Rams (10/16/88)*

On Bengals QB Boomer Esiason: Boomer tends to throw it hard. Boomer's a fastball pitcher. The biggest problem he's had in his career is being able to throw short. He looks deep, and he wants to throw deep all the time. The biggest adjustment he's had is to look deep and then throw short. And when you throw short at 120 miles-an-hour, it's hard to catch. *–Redskins at Bengals (12/17/88)*

On nervous quarterbacks: The way you can tell if a quarterback is nervous is by his feet. When his feet start moving quickly and jumping around, and he gets jumpy, that means that heart is pumping faster than it should be. –*Cowboys at Chargers (8/13/89)*

On Joe Montana's skill at throwing the slant pass: I think he throws that better than anyone's *ever* thrown it. He's probably thrown it so many times in his life that he can throw it with his eyes closed. Three steps – *Boom, Boom, Boom...Whap*! It's all in the timing. You can't get to him when you're on defense. –*Broncos at 49ers (8/19/89)*

On the Dolphins' tepid use of the running game: When you've got a gun like Dan Marino, you don't want to horse around with a lot of running. –*Eagles at Dolphins (9/2/89)*

On Giants QB Phil Simms overthrowing a receiver: I've always found that when a quarterback gets pumped up – when a quarterback plays a big game and you get an emotional guy like Phil Simms – they will tend to overthrow. They have so much adrenaline, and somehow that adrenaline just goes right into that arm early in the game. That's what we just saw. Phil Simms is so pumped up that he's having a hard time keeping the ball in the stadium. –*NFC Playoffs, Rams at Giants (1/7/90)*

On 49ers QB Joe Montana: I don't know that I've ever seen anyone do it any better than this guy does it. He just plays at a different level, another level. He makes it look so easy. The rest of the people...you struggle, you struggle through life to do things, and this guy comes in and makes a joke out of it. Even in practice. Everything he *does* is like that. –*NFC Championship Game, Rams at 49ers (1/14/90)*

On Rams QB Jim Everett dropping to the ground under phantom pressure: Everett felt the bullet when there were no bullets. I don't know that I've ever seen a quarterback get knocked down when there was no contact...You should *not* feel that. In this game, you gotta keep that head up and keep working to find a receiver or run it. You should not *feel* a guy behind you. –*NFC Championship Game, Rams at 49ers (1/14/90)*

On 49ers QB Joe Montana's majestic performances in Super Bowls: He's a remarkable quarterback. We used to talk about that before, saying he was the best in football. I don't think anyone even *argues* that anymore. Now we're on a level *Is he the best that ever played*? And I'm one that votes yes. –*Super Bowl XXIV, 49ers vs. Broncos (1/28/90)*

On 49ers QB Joe Montana: You talk about Montana at the start of a game, on the first drive, on how good he is. Then you talk about the end of the half, how good he is. Then you talk about the end of the game, how good he is. That's covering just about the whole pie. *–Redskins at 49ers (9/16/90)*

On second-year Cowboys QB Troy Aikman learning how to handle blitzes: One thing you learn as a young quarterback is how to read a blitz quickly and get rid of the ball. Because in your *first* year you're probably going to see more blitzes than any other quarterback. One thing you come out of that first year with is knowing what a blitz is, what it looks like, and you can feel when it's coming. *–Cowboys at Giants (9/30/90)*

On the Redskins' steady turnover at quarterback during the 1980s: The thing that bothers Joe Gibbs, he says, is "You look around and everyone has the same quarterback." Over a period of years, he's had like five or six quarterbacks, going back to Jay Schroeder and Doug Williams, Mark Rypien and Joe Theismann and Stan Humphries. He said, "Boy, would I like to have one like the 49ers, when you get a guy like Joe Montana for ten years. Or like Randall Cunningham. Every time I look up, there's Randall Cunningham on the other side. He's never hurt or never out." *–Eagles at Redskins (10/21/90)*

On Eagles QB Randall Cunningham throwing into a crowd: The difference between "confidence" and "forcing" is a very fine line. *–Packers at Eagles (12/16/90)*

On 49ers QB Joe Montana: Joe Montana is the coolest quarterback I've ever seen in my life. *–Saints at 49ers (12/23/90)*

On the repeated hits taken by Bears QB Mike Tomczak: When you wear a "teen" number, you're a marked man, especially when you have "QB" after your name. *–NFC Playoffs, Bears at Giants (1/13/91)*

On Giants backup QB Jeff Hostetler starting in the postseason: I've always said that a backup quarterback can win games, can even win playoff games, but I don't think he can win a championship, take you all the way to the Super Bowl. But the way this guy has played today, I don't know that I don't believe he couldn't do it. *–NFC Playoffs, Bears at Giants (1/13/91)*

On Bears QB Mike Tomczak: One of the Bear players told us something about Mike Tomczak and his confidence. He told us that the more he looks to the sidelines, the less confidence he has. It's really not fair to say that now it's 24-3. But he said that when Tomczak has a lot of confidence, he doesn't look at the sidelines as much. But when he doesn't have confidence, he's *always* looking over at the sidelines. *–NFC Playoffs, Bears at Giants (1/13/91)*

On Bears' inability to contain Giants QB Jeff Hostetler: The Bears have really had trouble keeping containment of Hostetler. If you take your outside guys and tell them to contain, a lot of times that takes the aggressiveness out of them. Then you just get 'em standing there. Then if you get 'em standing there, you say *Come on, go after him!* Then you go after him, and the quarterback goes outside. It drives you nuts. –*NFC Playoffs, Bears at Giants (1/13/91)*

On a hard hit taken by Bears QB Jim Harbaugh: Harbaugh had to stand in there because [DT] Ken Clarke was coming right up the middle. He had to step in and throw that one and *know* he was gonna get launched. When a quarterback takes a hit like that, there ought to be an airbag involved. –*Vikings at Bears (9/1/91)*

On Lions QB Erik Kramer's first NFL start: He does look like he has confidence out there…. Dave Levy, the offensive coordinator, was telling us last night, "This kid has cocky intelligence." I don't know what that means, but it sounds like something a quarterback should have. –*Lions at Bears (11/3/91)*

On a short throw to a running back by Redskins QB Mark Rypien: We were talking to Mark Rypien yesterday and we said, "What's the toughest throw to make?" He said, "The toughest throw to make is the back coming out of the backfield, running into the flat. It's easier to throw ins, outs, ups, deeps, anything because you get back and set. On that one, you never really get set to throw." –*Cowboys at Redskins (11/24/91)*

On Cowboys QB Troy Aikman writhing on the ground after a hard hit: He knows he's hurt, and I think he's more upset about *being* hurt than *hurt* by being hurt. –*Cowboys at Redskins (11/24/91)*

On Redskins QB Mark Rypien: When anyone thinks of touch, you always think of a short pass. But you also have to have a touch on a deep pass. No one has a better deep-pass touch than Mark Rypien of the Washington Redskins. –*Packers at Vikings (12/21/91)*

On veteran Chiefs QB Dave Krieg: You know what Dave Krieg does that few quarterbacks do today? On a running play, he carries out his fakes. That's one area of quarterbacking that has really gone downhill – the ball-handling part. Dave Krieg hands off and then he carries out a fake, so they always have to check him. And he can always check to see what they're gonna do against bootlegs. The good ones always do it. Bob Griese was great at it. –*Redskins at Chiefs (11/15/92)*

On Chiefs QB Dave Krieg: Dave Krieg is a streak passer. He's one of those guys who's either up or down. When he's good, he can really be good. And when he's bad, he can really be bad. He can throw a pretty good-looking pass, or he can throw some of the ugliest-looking passes that this league has ever seen. *–Redskins at Chiefs (11/15/92)*

On what QBs value most: The best friend of a quarterback is a good running game. *–Giants at Cowboys (11/26/92)*

On Broncos QB John Elway: Elway is someone who, at 40 yards, could throw it *through* a receiver when that shoulder and arm is healthy. You talk about a one-man gang, that guy is it. *–Cowboys at Broncos (12/6/92)*

On young Packers QB Brett Favre: Brett Favre is really an impressive guy, not only as a quarterback but as a field general. Just watching him out there on the field, you get a feeling of his presence. Although the coaches have the first 15 plays scripted and call them from the sideline, you have a feeling that this guy, even in his second year, really has control of this game... [Packers coach] Mike Holmgren was saying, "He's really like a linebacker out there. He's so fired up those first few plays you don't know what you're gonna get out of him." And Favre says, "Yeah, all I have to do is get some hits. I just have to get hit a few times, then I calm down and I'm ready to play." Any time you have a quarterback with the mentality of a linebacker, I think you have a heckuva player. *–Eagles at Packers (9/12/93)*

After a clumsy-looking pass by Eagles QB Randall Cunningham: Cunningham can do things with a football like a basketball player. That looked like kind of a half-pass, half-lateral, half-fumble. He kinda looked like he may have fumbled it. He kinda brings it back, then he [bobbles it], then he just throws a little pass to anyone...Throws it overhand, underhand. Left-footed. Yesterday we saw him out there kicking field goals. Kick it, throw it, do anything with that ball. *–Redskins at Eagles (9/19/93)*

On quarterbacks licking their fingers: Usually when quarterbacks lick their fingers, the next play is a pass. We used to always key on that. We used to call our plays and then watch the quarterback. If he'd come out and lick his fingers, all my guys would say "Pass!" Then you'd worry about the guy that would lick his fingers then call a draw or something. *–Giants at Cowboys (11/7/93)*

On Giants QB Phil Simms' skill at throwing the tight end seam: I don't know that anyone has ever thrown that pass better than Phil Simms. Remember that seam pass to Mark Bavaro all those years? That tight-ender right down the seam? You just get back there, hold it, pump, maybe look the other way, and throw the pass right up the field, right in stride. I don't think there's anyone who throws that seam pass better to a tight end, ever, than Phil Simms. –*Giants at Dolphins (12/5/93)*

On Dolphins QB Steve DeBerg: Steve DeBerg has had some great coaches. He started out with the Cowboys and had Tom Landry. He had Bill Walsh. He had Dan Reeves. In fact, when Dan Reeves was in Denver, he made a trade for Steve DeBerg. It came out in the news and his wife said, "What did you trade for DeBerg for?" Then they showed a picture of him coming to town on the nightly news and his wife said, "That's the best-looking guy I've ever seen! That's a great trade!" –*Giants at Dolphins (12/5/93)*

On Giants QB Phil Simms lifting weights: We were talking about Simms being so strong. He's a weightlifter. He lifts weights with *offensive linemen*. Now Dan Marino's on the other side. He doesn't lift weights. He's never worked out. [Simms] said he saw Marino and Marino hit him on the shoulder and said, "You're still lifting weights, hmm?" Simms said yeah. "Well, does it help you throw?" Simms said no. And Marino said, "Then what are you doing it for?" – *Giants at Dolphins (12/5/93)*

On the attire of Vikings QB Jim McMahon: He does everything that a quarterback shouldn't do. He wears a visor. How do you *see* through that thing? He wears gloves. How do you throw with *gloves* on? He has big old undershirts on under his uniform that you can't throw [while wearing]. He does it all wrong, and he still throws it out there. –*NFC Wildcard, Vikings at Giants (1/9/94)*

On the Cardinals offense repeatedly running on first and second down: That's the toughest kind of offense in football to play, where you run on first down and don't make enough, run on second down and don't make enough. Then you put in four wide receivers. The defense puts in seven defensive backs and they know you're gonna pass. They're gonna tee-off and you have to force it. For a quarterback, this is the toughest kind of offense you have to play. –*Cowboys at Cardinals (10/23/94)*

On the erratic play of Falcons QB Jeff George: He's been impressive today, but then he's really done some strange things. He'd probably drive you crazy if he's on your team, and he'd drive you crazy if you were defending him. –*Eagles at Falcons (11/27/94)*

On the QB sneak: I have never met a quarterback in my life that liked the quarterback sneak. –*49ers at Chargers (12/11/94)*

On Vikings QB Warren Moon drawing the Bears offside: Good quarterbacks make hard counts on third down. *–NFC Wildcard, Bears at Vikings (1/1/95)*

On coaching backup QBs: If I ever went back to coaching, I would have an assistant *just* to coach backup quarterbacks. I think it's *that* important. You need someone to coach those guys all the time.... The way football is today, you have so many situations that you have to practice, [which means] the starting quarterback gets all the practice plays. Backup quarterbacks should have their own coach and their own way to get prepared. *–49ers at Cowboys (11/12/95)*

On Cowboys QB Troy Aikman: Aikman's on a little hot streak here. They didn't get the first down, but he still completed the pass to Emmitt Smith. That was eleven straight. He gets that way. He'll get in a streak or in a zone or whatever that word is, and he can darn near get to perfect. *–Cowboys at Raiders (11/19/95)*

On Packers QB Brett Favre overthrowing his receivers at Texas Stadium: I think it's the crown of this field. This field in Dallas has the biggest crown there is. If you're on one hash mark, and you throw normal height to the other side, the ball is going to be high. I was talking to [backup QB] Jim McMahon about it yesterday. He said, "You've got to throw at a guy's knees to hit him in the shoulder. *–NFC Championship Game, Packers at Cowboys (1/14/96)*

On Dolphins QB Dan Marino: He's just a thing of beauty. I watch him and I'm mesmerized, the way he throws the ball.... He just has a gun. When he sees something, from the time he sees it until the ball gets there is a very short time. *–Cowboys at Dolphins (10/27/96)*

On Patriots QB Drew Bledsoe's skill at play-faking: I think that's part of having a dad as a head coach. He said he learned things like play-fake and screens before he learned how to use a knife and fork. *–Super Bowl XXXI, Packers vs. Patriots (1/26/97)*

On Packers QB Brett Favre delivering the bomb early in the Super Bowl: *That* is the way to settle down! Sometimes they think you have to start with short passes. I've always said when you've got a strong-armed guy and you want to settle him down and he's anxious, just throw a deep one! That's exactly what they did. *–Super Bowl XXXI, Packers vs. Patriots (1/26/97)*

On play-fakes by Packers QB Brett Favre: This is one of the reasons I vote for Brett Favre for MVP. He hands off, and then he goes back and he fakes that jump pass. No one has thrown a jump pass since Sid Luckman. I remember Sid Luckman and Charlie Trippi. Remember you used to get those bubble gum cards with the guy jumping up in the air and the hand out? No one has done that since, and now Brett Favre is bringing that back. *–Super Bowl XXXI, Packers vs. Patriots (1/26/97)*

On Packers QB Brett Favre: If there's such a thing as a fastball pitcher in football, that fastball pitcher is Brett Favre. *–49ers at Packers (11/1/98)*

On Dolphins QB Dan Marino's coolness after throwing a touchdown pass: He's done it so many times. That old thing where you throw a touchdown pass or score a touchdown, like he's done it before. There's nobody, other than Barry Sanders, that does better at "acting like they've done it before" than Dan Marino. Act like you've been there before, and you're gonna be there again. That's exactly how he does it. He plays football as a gentleman. *–Saints at Dolphins (11/29/98)*

On Rams QB Kurt Warner's first regular season appearance: SUMMERALL: [Coach] Dick Vermeil says in practice he just *scares* the defense. They can't stop him.

MADDEN: They gave him an award for Best Scout Team Player. Then Dick said he started getting him ready to play and it was totally different. He said [at running opposing team's plays] he was pretty good; at running the Ram offense against the [scout] defense, not so good. *–Rams at 49ers (12/27/98)*

NOTE: A year later, Warner was voted NFL MVP and Super Bowl MVP.

On Cardinals second-year QB Jake Plummer: He's the real deal. Jake Plummer is going to be a superstar in this league. You talk about the great quarterbacks. He is going to be – or has a heckuva chance to be – one of the next ones. *–NFC Playoffs, Cardinals at Vikings (1/10/99)*

NOTE: Plummer played ten years in the NFL, earning Pro Bowl honors just once. He was never voted All-Pro.

On the Rams' new QB sensation Kurt Warner: Marshall Faulk was talking about Kurt Warner. I asked him, "What did you think when Kurt Warner became the starting quarterback?" Faulk said, "How can *this* guy be the quarterback now when he's the guy they were yelling at all the time?" This is an old coach's thing. You coach your starting quarterback *through* your backup quarterback by yelling at *him*. Trent Green was the quarterback; Kurt Warner was the backup, so they just yelled at him so that Trent Green could hear it. Now Kurt Warner is the starter, and they don't yell at him anymore. *–Rams at 49ers (11/21/99)*

On the Rams QB Kurt Warner learning to stay in the pocket: He said when he was a freshman quarterback in high school, they had a drill with no receivers. He'd go back to pass, and the drill was called "Kill Kurt." They'd just run right at him and into him, and that's how he learned to stand in there.... I don't know too many who'd come back for their sophomore year.... That's what Kurt Warner learned years ago in that "Kill Kurt" drill, that there's gonna be guys flying at you but you don't let 'em bother you. –*NFC Playoffs, Vikings at Rams (1/16/00)*

On 158 being the highest possible quarterback rating: 158 is a funny number for perfect. –*NFC Playoffs, Vikings at Rams (1/16/00)*

On Rams QB Kurt Warner: Vikings coach Denny Green was saying last night – and it's so true – that Kurt Warner, at hitting guys on the run, where they don't have to break stride, is the best since Joe Montana. –*Vikings at Rams (12/10/00)*

On potential of new 49ers QB Jeff Garcia: I have to confess – I didn't see it. I went to a practice when Jeff Garcia was in mini-camp, and Bill Walsh says, "Take a look at him and tell me what you think." He was the *worst* practice player I'd ever seen. I thought he couldn't play. Bill didn't ask me [for my opinion] after that practice. –*Eagles at 49ers (11/25/02)*

On Titans workhorse QB Steve McNair, who played at 6-2, 235lbs: You usually don't say that about a quarterback, but Steve McNair is a load...He's so big and thick. If you go to tackle that body, tackling him is more like tackling a big, old fullback like Larry Csonka than it is a quarterback. –*Patriots at Titans (12/16/02)*

More on McNair: He is something very, very special. If you're gonna win, you jump on his shoulders. –*Patriots at Titans (12/16/02)*

NOTE: Despite Madden's enthusiasm, McNair was never voted first-team All-Pro during his 13-year career; he made second-team once, in 2002.

On Giants QB Kerry Collins' reputation as a starter: Kerry Collins, to me, has always been a slow starter. It takes him a while to get into the game. You hope by the time he gets into it, it's not already over for him. –*Giants at Buccaneers (11/24/03)*

On Patriots QB Tom Brady being compared to Joe Montana: When people say that Tom Brady is a lot like Joe Montana, I think it's just his coolness. You get third down, he has to roll out, he doesn't have a lot of speed. But he knows where to go, how to set his feet, how to find the open guy and how to put the ball right on him. He's so cool. I was talking to [Colts coach] Tony Dungy last night. We were talking about Brady, and he said "There's three things a quarterback has to do: He has to have poise, he has to be accurate, and he has to be intelligent." He said his quarterback, Peyton

Manning is that, but he also said Tom Brady's like that. *–Colts at Patriots (9/9/04)*

On Patriots QB Tom Brady being fourth-string during his rookie year: For over half the games, he didn't even dress. He was up in the stands. You have your first two quarterbacks, then you have your third or emergency quarterback, and your fourth quarterback is like a nothing. Bill Belichick was saying last night, if he had a team like he has now, he couldn't afford to keep a fourth quarterback. He said, "We were so bad [in 2000], we could have cut the team to 48. We could've cut it to 45. We could've cut the team to 35 at that time." So, if you don't have a good team, it's easier to keep a guy like Tom Brady as your fourth quarterback. *–Patriots at Dolphins (12/20/04)*

On Packers QB Brett Favre: Every offensive player comes alive when Brett Favre is the quarterback. *–Vikings at Packers (11/21/05)*

On Steelers QB Ben Roethlisberger's ability to fight off a pass rush: That's when he's at his best. Seattle defensive coordinator John Marshall said, "Guys just drip off him." What I also like about him is he stays alive. He flipped that one out there underhand to Hines Ward. He keeps looking downfield, trying to make a play in the passing game and not running with the ball. *–Super Bowl XL, Steelers vs. Seahawks (2/5/06)*

Comparing Tom Brady to Peyton Manning as signal callers: MADDEN: Brady started his count, then had to go back and identify the middle linebacker. He is so *calm* doing that.

AL MICHAELS: Manning-like.

MADDEN: I think Brady's *calmer* than Peyton Manning. Peyton Manning stops his cadence, starts a new cadence, moves a guy around, identifies the middle linebacker. He kinda makes you nervous, like you just had three pots of coffee. *–Chargers at Patriots (9/16/07)*

Chapter 3: RUNNING BACKS

Cowboys tailback Tony Dorsett turns it on against the Rams.

On Buccaneers RB Jerry Eckwood botching an inside running play: That's one thing that Jerry Eckwood, a rookie, will learn. When you have an inside running play to the strong side, you really have to keep it inside. You can't bounce it outside because you don't have a blocker for the strong safety. *–Packers at Buccaneers (10/21/79)*

More on Eckwood: Eckwood has had some fumbling problems this year. He's a rookie, and of course he has the cast on his wrist. The other thing is, he really fights for yardage. I would take that anytime. Sometimes you're gonna get some fumbles, but when a guy will twist and turn and fight to get those extra yards, sometimes it's worth it. *–Packers at Buccaneers (10/21/79)*

On Falcons tailback Lynn Cain: He played at USC for my friend John Robinson. John coached with me at Oakland. We grew up together. John told me about Lynn Cain. He said, "He's your type of running back. You ought to draft him." I retired and never had a chance. John never gave me anything before that, but when I retired he told me about Lynn Cain. He was right! *–Falcons at Patriots (9/14/80)*

On undervalued backs like Raiders Pete Banaszak: Every year you go to camp and you're gonna cut him. The next thing, you start playing and he's playing your short yardages. He's playing your special teams. He's winning games for you. He's one of the most valuable players on your team *–Lions at Chiefs (10/26/80)*

On Eagles tailback Wilbert Montgomery: He has great feet. The definition of great feet is that the two of them work together, and they never get in spread-out or elongated positions. It's the same thing with hands. What are good hands? Both hands working together. *–Eagles at Redskins (11/16/80)*

On Cardinals RB Ottis Anderson: I like Ottis Anderson a lot more from the I-formation. When he lines up in a split backfield, he has to run all the way across the backfield, where he has yet to turn his shoulders and get 'em up square. Ottis Anderson is best when he is into the secondary with his shoulders square. *–Cardinals at Giants (11/30/80)*

On why great runners are most dangerous in the open field: That's when they can see better. They can cut either way – right or left. Before they get [into open field], they can't make those right or left cuts. *–Cardinals at Giants (11/30/80)*

On running backs being pulled down by their jerseys: That's why there were some running backs in the league putting Vaseline on their jerseys. But the thing you worry about is that they go out to catch a pass and the ball goes through and hits the Vaseline and they fumble. So, you don't know whether to use it or not. *–Falcons at Eagles (12/7/80)*

On why some running backs are more effective in second half: Early in the game they have some nervousness, some anxiety, and the defense is a little quicker. Then the defense gets run down, [backs] get a little tired and they *lose* that anxiety. Then they just go to pure instinct and running. *–Lions at Chiefs (10/26/80)*

On Bears tailback Walter Payton: The thing that impressed me about Walter Payton is when he talks about records and himself, he says "we." He always includes his offensive line. He says, "We're happy that we're here...We wanna do this...We'll be happy when we do that...." It's always "we." And a *true* "we." *–Bears at Buccaneers (12/20/80)*

On Redskins RB Terry Metcalf's severe fumbling problem: A lot of people say concentration...They say they have the ball out...I don't believe any of those things. I think people that have *small hands* tend to fumble more than people with long hands and strong hands and fingers. I think Metcalf doesn't have those big bones in his wrists and those big hands. *–Giants at Redskins (9/13/81)*

On running the ball late in the game with a lead: You don't want your backs to fight for yardage *now* because you don't want a fumble. *–Rams at Giants (12/6/81)*

On Packers RB Gerry Ellis: Gerry Ellis is a big strong guy. He weighs about 220 pounds. I was asking him last night, "As a running back do you recover by Wednesday or Thursday?" He said no, he really doesn't recover until Saturday. He plays on Sunday, then the next time he feels good or feels normal is the next Saturday. That's a long time to recover! You can see why Gerry Ellis feels that way. It's because he runs straight-up and they get a lot of shots at him. *–Giants at Packers (11/8/81)*

On great RBs: Great running backs can smell the end zone. *–Eagles at Cowboys (12/13/81)*

On the running game: One thing about the running game, it takes a little while to get it going. You have to slow down or wear down that defense, and then you get it going in the third and fourth quarter. *–Giants at Eagles (11/22/81)*

After a surging run by Oilers RB Earl Campbell: Look at this move here, that little cutback. He even looks good when he stumbles. Look at that power. Those legs keep driving. Boy, is he hard to bring down! Head's up...shoulders are always square. *–Falcons at Oilers (11/29/81)*

On fumbling: Great running backs tend to have more fumbles than average running backs. Why? Because they have good balance, and they're always fighting for yardage. *–Falcons at Oilers (11/29/81)*

On Cowboys RB Tony Dorsett: Dorsett is one of those type of running back that's like Russian Roulette. You stop them, you stop them...but you can never feel comfortable that you have his number. You know there are still some shots in there that could finish the day for you. *–Eagles at Cowboys (12/13/81)*

On Eagles RB Wilbert Montgomery: He really takes a lot of hits because he's not a real good avoid-runner. He breaks tackles, runs though things, and as a result he gets hit much more than some of them. *–NFC Wildcard, Giants at Eagles (12/27/81)*

On bruising Jets fullback Mike Augustyniak: There's the type of guy you like to see play. He went to Purdue as a walk-on; he didn't have a scholarship and made the team. He wasn't drafted by anyone. *Waived...cut...bring him back.* Last year he had a very serious injury and missed half the year. Those determined guys. Look at him! His neck is bigger than his ears! When your neck comes outside your ears, that's a big neck...Augustyniak looks like a bull in a china closet. *–Buccaneers at Jets (12/12/82)*

On Rams FB Mike Guman being stopped at goal line: I love football on the goal line, but one thing [must be stressed]: You have to take that ball and keep it going forward! Now watch Guman. He delays right there a little and tries to bounce out. You *cannot* delay when you're running on the goal line. You can't delay. *–Rams at Raiders (12/18/82)*

After a short burst by Giants RB Rob Carpenter: Before that last play to Carpenter, we saw [coach] Ray Perkins signal the play in. He had about ten things he was doing – hitting his chest, head, boom-boom, the whole thing. And all it was, was a fullback right up the middle. Remember in the old days you used to say "Gimme a plunge on two?" Now they go *Boom-Boom-Boom*. *–Giants at Eagles (1/2/83)*

On Dallas RB Tony Dorsett: That's what I like about Dorsett – he doesn't run out of bounds. As a coach, I used to *hate* that. I used to tell them, "Anyone can run out of bounds. When you get to that sideline, you have to turn it up and finish off the run." This guy does it. He does a lot of tough things. You think of him and those quick things...catching the ball, sweeps and such. But he does a lot of those tough-type things. *–NFC Playoffs, Packers at Cowboys (1/16/83)*

On Redskins RB John Riggins' opinion of drawing plays on chalkboards: About those coaches' meetings where they go and draw plays on the blackboard, John Riggins was saying, "I don't pay any attention to that stuff. It never looks the same on the field as it does on the blackboard. The only place it's important is how it looks during the game." *–NFC Championship Game, Cowboys at Redskins (1/22/83)*

On Giants RB Rob Carpenter: I think Carpenter is one of those guys that you really have to work...You have to *give him the ball, give him the ball, give him the ball*. Mark van Eeghen used to be that way for me. He was a better player when he was tired. After his first 15 carries, he'd start to run like a real fullback. On those first fifteen, he was never as good. He had too much nervousness. *–Giants at Cowboys (9/18/83)*

On rookie RB Eric Dickerson's unique running style: Bill Parcells said he's a skipper, one of those guys that can skip. I know what he means. I think we see it right here. It's a delay play, a draw. See that little skip in there? *Another* skip in there. There's only about two or three guys that ever played this game that had those skips. You don't teach that. They're born with that. –*Rams at Giants (9/4/83)*

On Rams RB Eric Dickerson's uniform number: 29 is a funny number for him. I told [coach] John Robinson I don't like that number. He said, "You will after you watch him play. Some guys carry good numbers, and some guys *make* good numbers." –*Rams at Giants (9/4/83)*

On Dallas tailback Tony Dorsett: That guy right there, Tony Dorsett, is a pretty good juker. Tom Landry was saying he's *not* a blaster. That's why they get him so deep in the backfield, to let that defense react. By the time Dorsett gets there, he just runs *against* their reaction. –*Giants at Cowboys (9/18/83)*

On fumbling problem of Rams rookie RB Eric Dickerson: In the first three games, he had six fumbles. That's one thing you really can't coach, nor can you coach *against*. It's really something you can't talk about because they don't try to do it. And if you start talking about it, then they get so conscious [of it]. Dickerson said, "If I start thinking about it, then I would become robotic." –*Rams at Jets (9/25/83)*

On Jets' "third-down" back Bruce Harper: That's an interesting thing, Bruce Harper being in there on first down. He's called the third-down back. The Jets have first-down backs, second-down backs, third-down backs and short-yardage backs. Bruce Harper is a third-down back who was in there on first down. That could confuse one that didn't understand it. *Sometimes we put our third-down backs in on first down.* Yeah, heck, *I* understand that deal. –*Falcons at Jets (10/23/83)*

On Cowboys RB Timmy Newsome inadvertently stepping out of bounds after a long run: He has plenty of room to *not* step out of bounds. He just ran right out of bounds! I used to have a drill for that. I used to drill my players into a fence. I'd say, "That's the sideline," so they always had to cut up. If they wanted to run out of bounds, they'd run into the fence... I think Newsome needs the old fence drill. If you *really* want to be tough, you make it a brick wall. –*Cowboys at Eagles (11/6/83)*

On fullbacks "moving the sticks": That's what a fullback should do. They keep all those stats, how many average yards per carry and all that stuff. But for a fullback the important things you do are short-yardage and goal-line.

You run that other stuff for show, but you do that short-yardage and goal-line for dough. That's the important stuff. *–Redskins at Giants (11/13/83)*

On burly, unshaven Redskins RB John Riggins: If you're a Hog and a fullback, you don't shave and stuff like that. You don't eat fruit and crackers. *–Redskins at Cowboys (12/11/83)*

On a 16-yard, second-half burst by Redskins RB John Riggins: This is the reason that a fullback does so well in the second half of a game. The defense gets a little tired. They're not as quick, they're not as strong, they've been beaten down by this big offensive line all day. They don't tackle the same way at the end of the game as they do at the beginning of the game. A fullback will always pop bigger runs in the second half than he does in the first half. *–NFC Playoffs, Rams at Redskins (1/1/84)*

On Redskins RB John Riggins spitting out a sip of water: He even spits like a fullback and a Hog, you see that? You just spit and let it go right down the front of your shirt…Isn't that a good Hog spit, the way he's spitting? It just goes and dribbles down. A quarterback, like Theismann, if he were gonna spit it would go out in front of him. They'd make it go out and hit the ground. [Hogs] don't worry about it. You *get* a little on your jersey. *–NFC Playoffs, Rams at Redskins (1/1/84)*

On the 1983 NFC Championship game: John Riggins was telling us the other day that that 49er game, that championship game he played two weeks ago, may have been the toughest game he ever played. He said he had divots all over his body. He said he got some of them replaced, but it just doesn't look the same after they're replaced. *–Super Bowl XVIII, Redskins vs. Raiders (1/22/84)*

On Marcus Allen's riveting 74-yard touchdown run: You don't teach that kind of running. This is reaction. This is a great running back…You don't teach that. You don't practice that. You don't see that on films. That *happens*. *–Super Bowl XVIII, Redskins vs. Raiders (1/22/84)*

On Bears RB Walter Payton: That Walter Payton is an amazing guy…When he runs inside, he runs like a fullback. When he runs outside, he runs like a halfback. When he goes out for a pass, he runs like a wide receiver. And when he blocks, he blocks like a guard. That's a pretty good combination…He *really* has a body on him. We saw him yesterday. He is so big and compact and strong. Amazing guy. They made a pretty good deal there when they made him. *–Cowboys at Bears (9/30/84)*

On Redskins fullback John Riggins playing at RFK Stadium: I think Riggins was made for football. But I think he was made for *this* type of football, *this* team, playing in *this* stadium on grass. I couldn't see him playing on one of those plastic turfs in a big stadium out by an airport someplace. – *Cowboys at Redskins (10/14/84)*

On Redskins fullback John Riggins: When he hits those piles, they go backwards. That's what the fullbacks do. The halfback and tailbacks, you want them to run around. Fullbacks? You want them to make piles go backwards. –*Redskins at Cowboys (12/9/84)*

On Cardinals punishing RB Ottis Anderson: He's a big guy, isn't he? Most halfbacks try to juke you or run around you. Ottis Anderson is one that loves to punish you, to run over you. To find a guy – a safety – that he can hit and hurt. When they played Philadelphia, they had a real *thing* going. Wes Hopkins is their hard-hitting safety. Every time Ottis Anderson would break in the clear, he'd try to find Hopkins to run over. –*Cardinals at Redskins (12/16/84)*

On a camera shot of Redskins RB John Riggins on the bench: Now *there's* a fullback. You got a little sweat on ya, a towel over your head. You don't shave to play…. You just finish the oxygen after you get a touchdown. A little smile. You don't keep it there long, though. Fullback. –*Cardinals at Redskins (12/16/84)*

On Redskins 5-10 RB Joe Washington: Joe Gibbs always calls him The Little Guy…*The Little Guy's dinged, The Little Guy hasn't played, The Little Guy this and that*. That was fine last year. This year they got [5-9] Keith Griffin, and Gibbs calls *him* The Little Guy. So, when he says, "The Little Guy this and that," you don't know who he's talking about – Joe Washington or Keith Griffin? –*Cardinals at Redskins (12/16/84)*

On a replay of Bears tailback Walter Payton: The great thing about a Walter Payton is you really don't have to block everyone. You can block about five or six and he'll get by the other two or three. Watch him on this. He has his off guard and off tackle pulling in front. He makes a guy miss there, makes a miss here, cuts back. You block half, then he'll take on the *other* half of your defense. –*NFC Championship Game, Bears at 49ers (1/6/85)*

On a goal-line fumble by Giants' rookie George Adams: This is why, as a coach, I always worried about letting a rookie player have the ball on the goal line. There's always gonna be a bunch of bodies in there. Guys are gonna be grabbing the ball, knocking it out. You need that veteran guy who can cinch it up, put it away, so that it can't get popped out while he's jumping over the pile. That's what happened to George Adams there. –*Giants at Eagles (9/29/85)*

On underperforming Giants RB Tony Galbreath: Bill Parcells had a talk with Tony Galbreath this week. He said, "You know, when we put you in there on third down, we haven't been very successful at that. Really, that's all you do. So, if you don't do well when it's *all* you do, then we won't need you much longer." –*Buccaneers at Giants (11/3/85)*

On high-stepping style of 49ers Roger Craig: Craig has that high-knee action…You see how those legs are going and churning? And when he gets grabbed, he never stops. He keeps those legs going – *Boom! Boom! Boom! Boom! Boom*! And he breaks so many tackles by that. –*49ers at Redskins (12/1/85)*

On image of Cowboys veteran Tony Dorsett: You always think of Tony Dorsett as a young guy, but he's been there for *nine years*. Then, you always think the other way, like he's *always* been there. A young guy who's always been there! –*Cowboys at 49ers (12/22/85)*

On prospects of Cowboys Tony Dorsett and Herschel Walker playing in the same backfield: I think they can both play. I think they can both help the team, but I wonder how they can both play in the same backfield. I think that's something that's more fun to *talk* about than it ever is in reality…It's nice to have two of them. One can come out, the other one goes in fresh, but I don't think you'll ever use them both at the same time as a big part of your offense. –*Cardinals at Bears (8/23/86)*

On Cowboys RB Tony Dorsett avoiding hard hits: There's not one running back that's better at avoiding that direct, flush contact than Tony Dorsett. He always made you kinda miss and just skim him when you hit him. –*Cowboys at Broncos (10/5/86)*

On versatility of Cowboys RB Herschel Walker*:* I was watching tapes with [Giants RB] Ottis Anderson the other night. Walker was out as a wide receiver and the defensive back was about twenty yards off him. He looked at Herschel Walker and said, "*That's* what it does." I said, "What's *that*?" He said, "That's what *speed* does." That's the thing about Walker; you can put him any place – fullback, halfback, wide receiver. Put him any place and he can come up with a big play. –*Cowboys at Giants (11/2/86)*

On Cowboys RB Tony Dorsett: I think Tony Dorsett is the best back that ever ran a screen pass in football, in the history of the game. I can see him running the screen where he gets out there. He lets his linemen get out in front of him, picks that hole, then gets that thing into the open field. Tony Dorsett has been doing that for ten years for this team. I don't think anyone has ever done it better. –*Bears at Cowboys (12/21/86)*

A physics lesson on Giants tailback Joe Morris: MADDEN: We were talking about Joe Morris earlier in the season, and I was talking about physics. Joe Morris is *not* a little guy. Joe Morris is a *big* guy. He's just short. He has big, powerful arms, shoulders, legs and the whole thing. Physics. I thought if you take your power – you weigh around 200 pounds – and you keep it short, that that would be *stronger* than someone who was the same weight but taller. Anyway, I got a lot of letters on that.

SUMMERALL: Well, it makes a lot of sense.

MADDEN: What it is, is mass times velocity equals power. Morris has the record for mass and velocity under 5-6. He has 190-some pounds in about 5-6. That power is shortened down, so you get more power spread over less area. That's called the mass. When he runs, that's called the velocity that equals the power. –*NFC Playoffs, 49ers at Giants (1/4/87)*

More on Giants RB Joe Morris: I finally got that power thing right. Raul Allegre, the kicker for the Giants, is an engineer. He told me what the formula is. It's power equals force times distance over time. So that's what Morris has. He has force times distance over time – and that's why he has so much power. –*NFC Championship Game, Redskins at Giants (1/11/87)*

After a short run by Saints replacement player Jeff Rodenberger: Saints coach Jim Mora said, "Ol' Rodenberger, he's good for a half-a-yard any time you need it." How'd you like to be known for that – half a yard? *Ol' Half-yard Rodenberger*. I guess it depends on how much you need. If you need ten yards, half a yard is bad; a couple of inches, half a yard is great. That's specialization. –*Saints at Bears (10/18/87)*

On Packers RB Brent Fullwood's nose for the endzone: Fullwood is a rookie number one draft choice who doesn't start, and his special place is on the goal line. [Coach] Forrest Gregg says he just has a feeling for getting yards in short-yardage situations.... Some people have a feel for goal-line offense. That's what Fullwood has. *Somewhere* there'll be a soft spot. He jumps, he dives, he hurdles, he goes sideways and finds that soft spot that will put him in the endzone. Some people know how to move their bodies. Look how he dives then moves sideways! That little move where you don't go in there square and give those linebackers something to dive on. –*Bears at Packers (11/8/87)*

On Bears RB Walter Payton's decline in productivity: I think he's struggling a little right now, and I think Mike Ditka is struggling with *that*.

Mike Ditka knows that Payton has lost a step. But he's been such a great player and such a great Bear for so long that he really doesn't want to do anything about it. –*Bears at Packers (11/8/87)*

On the impact of Giants FB Maurice Carthon: You can't tell me that he doesn't make a difference. He doesn't have the stats. It's not gonna look good in the statistics, but he gives this team some toughness. It looks like everyone gets picked up: The line blocks better. Joe Morris runs better. The whole thing has a better feel about it for the Giants than when he's *not* in there. [FB] George Adams may be faster, may be a better receiver and all those things, but you need a couple of tough guys in there. –*Giants at Redskins (11/29/87)*

On former Bills fullback Cookie Gilchrist: Cookie Gilchrist may have been the best blocking fullback to ever play the game. –*NFC Wildcard, Vikings at Saints (1/3/88)*

On undersized Vikings RB Darrin Nelson: Darrin Nelson is running so hard and fast today that he has to tape his pants on. You gotta like that. You're going, you got those hips moving, that stuff's moving in the lower legs, and you're just gonna fly right out of your pants. You're gonna *pants* yourself. That's what the tape's for. –*NFC Wildcard, Vikings at Saints (1/3/88)*

On Rams RB Greg Bell "finishing off a run": One of the things that [Rams coach] John Robinson teaches is "finish off your runs." Watch Greg Bell here. He knows he's going to be tackled, so he squares up and finishes it off. *Get their pile going backwards. Pick up another couple yards while you're going down.* As John says, the worst thing a running back can do is run at angles. –*Rams at Giants (9/25/88)*

On the dynamic style of 49ers RB Roger Craig: He has that thing of getting those knees high and keeping the shoulders low! He makes every team look like they're bad tacklers, the way he gets that high knee-action and keeps those feet going like two pistons. At the same time that the knees are going high, the shoulder can get low to take on the tackler. That's an amazing ability this guy has. –*49ers at Rams (10/16/88)*

On a short TD run by 49ers RB Roger Craig, as he churns over a pile of bodies: He keeps his shoulders square going upfield, he keeps his knees high, and he keeps his feet going. He never stops the feet. The feet never get planted. You never have anything stationary to tackle. Those feet are always going in and out of the ground. The knees are going up and the shoulders are down. An amazing combination of what you can do with a body. He kicks out of tackles even when there's no tackler around. –*49ers at Rams (10/16/88)*

On Roger Craig's workout regimen: Roger Craig is one of those guys that works out in the offseason three times a day. He runs distances. The thing that he said helps him the most is running hills and inclines. He said, "That's the way you can learn to lift your knees high and keep your shoulders down – by running up a hill." I tried it last night walking, and I can see what he means. *–49ers at Rams (10/16/88)*

On 49ers fullback Tom Rathman: There's an old-fashioned fullback. He's a guy who looked like he would've played for the Green Bay Packers under Vince Lombardi. He *runs* like a fullback. They talk about the Forty-Niners being a finesse team. Baloney! Watch this trap, and then watch Rathman. I'll guarantee you, this is *not* finesse running. This is old Nebraska football running. Old Green Bay Packer running. I would've loved to have had Tom Rathman play for me. I had guys like that [in Oakland]. Pete Banaszak was like Tom Rathman, one of those tough guys. Marv Hubbard was like that. Mark van Eeghen. Those are tough guys that give everything they have and are always looking for something or someone to hit. *–NFC Championship, 49ers at Bears (1/8/89)*

On 49ers RBs Tom Rathman and Roger Craig: They have a deal. Tom Rathman, who blocks all the time for Craig, was walking off the practice field with Craig. Rathman comes up to Craig and jumps on his shoulders, the old piggyback thing. And Craig carries him *off the field*! I said, "What's the deal?" Rathman said that he blocks for Craig all the time during the game, so after practice Craig has to carry Rathman off the field. That's a good gimmick. Some guys give [their blockers] money, they give them presents. You give him a piggyback ride! *–Broncos at 49ers (8/19/89)*

On poor running style of Dolphins FB Tom Brown: I think he has to keep his feet going a little more. He has a big upper body, but he stops driving his feet too soon. He stops driving his feet with contact. I would make him, on contact, go *BOOM!* Then you make those feet go *whap-whap-whap-whap*. I think he goes *BOOM!* then forgets the *whap-whap-whap-whap* with the feet. That can be taught. That can be drilled. That's an easy one to teach. *Keep those feet going, man! –Eagles at Dolphins (9/2/89)*

On Cowboys RB Broderick Sargent pulling a hamstring after a long run: That's like driving a car and getting a flat tire. Or getting a blowout. *–Eagles at Cowboys (11/23/89)*

On Rams RB Greg Bell: Greg Bell is one of those guys that's built for this type of [muddy] field, because there's not a lot of him to hit. And most of the stuff that he *has* to hit has pads on it. He just pulls all those pads together and you hit plastic-against-plastic. Unless you wrap up, you tend to bounce off him. *–NFC Championship Game, Rams at 49ers (1/14/90)*

On Packers RB Michael Haddix: There's a guy that's a heady player. He's what [coach] Lindy Infante calls his "flush" back. When they use four wide receivers for a passing formation, that's called "flush." The back that goes in with them is called the "flush" back. How'd you like to be the mother of the flush back? What's your kid doing? *Well, he's up there in Green Bay playing "flush." –Rams at Packers (9/9/90)*

On artistry of Lions RB Barry Sanders: Sometimes you just have to look at something and enjoy it. There's *no one* else in football that can make these moves...The moves he makes and the way he runs is just an art form. *–Lions at Seahawks (12/30/90)*

On Barry Sanders being used as a blocker: I'll tell ya, if I ever had Barry Sanders, Barry Sanders would *never* block. I would always have another blocking back in there to lead for him. Or I would have a tight end in there to block for *him*. *–Lions at Seahawks (12/30/90)*

On Saints RB Dalton Hilliard: When you think of the tough guys in the league, the tough tacklers, you think of [49ers safety] Ronnie Lott. He told me once that the toughest guy to tackle is Dalton Hilliard. He said that Hilliard is the toughest running back in the National Football League, "that he has so much power in those legs that when he hits you, he knocks everything right out of you." *–NFC Wildcard, Saints at Bears (1/6/91)*

On Raiders RB Roger Craig's upright running style: When you get into the third and fourth quarter, he always looks like a warrior because he goes in there and gives you everything to hit. Some guys get down and you have nothing but helmet, shoulder pads and knees. Craig gives you a lot of [jersey] number to hit, and a lot of waist, and a lot of thigh to hit. *–49ers at Raiders (9/29/91)*

On Cowboys RB Emmitt Smith: We were talking to [guard] Nate Newton last week and he was saying the toughest thing is when, "They call the play and it's supposed to come to your hole and Smith goes way over on the other side. Then sometimes you think it's going to the *other* side and you want to take a little rest, and he comes right back to your hole." What he's saying is, when Emmitt Smith is in there – as a big ol' 330-pound offensive tackle – you have to play every down. *–NFC Playoffs, Cowboys at Lions (1/5/92)*

On Barry Sanders giving a rare high-five after a touchdown: After he does something like that, everyone around him gets excited. This is about as much you get out of him. Barry Sanders does not throw the ball. He doesn't dance. He doesn't do spikes. He does nothing. He said when he scores, his feeling is one of relief. He said once in college he raised his hand up after a touchdown and he didn't like it. He hasn't done anything since. *–NFC Playoffs, Cowboys at Lions (1/5/92)*

On Chiefs rampaging fullback Christian Okoye: If you're ever gonna stop Christian Okoye, you'd better get him in his own backfield, before he gets to the line of scrimmage. He hardly ever goes to the outside. He usually runs between the tackles...When you get Okoye into the secondary, at 260 pounds, he's gonna always make six, seven or eight yards. *–Redskins at Chiefs (11/15/92)*

On 49ers fullback Tom Rathman playing hurt: He said an interesting thing yesterday. He said that he's "playing hurt and getting healthy." That's an oxymoron, I think. But if there's anyone that can do it, it's Tom Rathman. What it means is, you play hurt. And if you don't get hurt anymore, then you'll get healthy. He says it's worked. He played hurt and got healthy. Someone ought to write that one on a wall. *–Eagles at 49ers (11/29/92)*

After a blistering hit by Mike Singletary on Cowboys RB Emmitt Smith: Did you see Emmitt Smith? He didn't even look at Singletary. He took that hit, and one thing about running backs and guys that get hit – you *don't* acknowledge the hit. I mean, Singletary really unloaded on him. Emmitt Smith just gets up and he doesn't even look back. He doesn't look at Singletary. He doesn't look at anyone. He just goes right back to the huddle. I think average players talk a lot; I think *great* players just go back to the huddle, like a great fighter going back to his corner. *–Bears at Cowboys (12/27/92)*

On the high energy level of 49ers RB Ricky Watters: He's a fun guy. He's brought a lot of running to this team, and he's brought a lot of life to it, too. He's the guy that everyone kids in practice, and he kids everyone in practice. That guy has more energy than any ten players on this team. He reminds me of a whirling dervish. But I don't know what that is... He said that all week the players were telling him *Our backs are up against the wall...It's a short season...It's a new season...Super Bowl.* He said, "What am I gonna do different? I only know one way to play. What am I supposed to do? I can't get any higher than I get."*–NFC Playoffs, Redskins at 49ers (1/9/93)*

On 49ers RB Ricky Watters' "spin" move: There's nobody better at spinning than Ricky Watters. Anyone can go out there and spin but knowing *when* to do it and *how* to do it takes a special guy. Sometimes coaches don't like you to do that. They like you to finish off your run, to get behind your shoulder pads and do those types of things, but don't spin! But if you have a talent like Ricky Watters, you'd better use it. –*NFC Championship Game, Cowboys at 49ers (1/17/93)*

On 49ers RB Ricky Watters' tantrum after a fumble: You're upset with yourself because you fumbled, then you get upset with anyone who *talks* to you about being upset...Everyone's trying to calm him down, and you *have* to calm him down before you give him the ball again. –*NFC Championship Game, Cowboys at 49ers (1/17/93)*

After a key block by Cowboys FB Daryl Johnston: That's why these fullbacks are so valuable, whether you're talking about Johnston on the Cowboys or Rathman on the 49ers. They don't have a lot of the glory things, but they make the glory things available to the other guys. –*NFC Championship Game, Cowboys at 49ers (1/17/93)*

On Eagles rookie RB Vaughn Hebron: Hebron draws a crowd. He said that anytime he played in the preseason, guys were saying the regular season is up a notch. He said, "It could be up a notch, but to me it's just another guy trying to get me...I get the ball whether it's a scrimmage, or it's a preseason game or a regular season game. It's just guys trying to *get* me." –*Redskins at Eagles (9/19/93)*

On Rams rookie tailback Jerome Bettis: He's a big guy. He has the size of a fullback. He's darn near the size of a guard, but he runs like a tailback. He has some moves. He has movement, too. He has movement, with a load, and that's a pretty good combination. –*Rams at 49ers (10/31/93)*

On 260-lb running back Ironhead Heyward: He has real soft hands and he has soft feet. He's just a heavy guy that's a running back. He's not a guard. He's not a tackle. He looks like a guard or a nose tackle. But he's a running back in a nose tackle's body. And when he gets that load going up the field, you better tackle him low. We were talking to [LB] Pat Swilling, who played with him in New Orleans, and he said, "One thing I told all the guys: Don't try to tackle him high. If you try to tackle Ironhead Heyward high, you're gonna lose that battle." –*Bears at Lions (11/25/93)*

On Lions tailback Barry Sanders: We were talking a week ago to Carlton Bailey, who's a linebacker for the New York Giants. It was about the toughest back you have to play against. He said, "It's Barry Sanders. Every time I play against Barry Sanders, the next day I have groin pulls in both legs." It's from trying to change directions quickly, and you end up doing the splits. –*Bears at Lions (11/25/93)*

On Giants scatback Dave Meggett: Dave Meggett is one of those guys who can break tackles before he gets to a hole and then while he's *in* the hole. There are a lot of runners who make moves *before* they get into a hole and make moves when they get *out* of the hole, but they don't make 'em *in* the hole. He's one of the few that does. –*Giants at Dolphins (12/5/93)*

On Cowboys tailback Emmitt Smith: I think Emmitt Smith is one of the greatest cutback runners that's ever played this game. –*Cowboys at Vikings (12/12/93)*

On difference between 49ers tailbacks Amp Lee and Ricky Watters: The one difference between Amp Lee and Ricky Watters is Watters is a bigger, stronger, more physical guy. Ricky Watters can run through things…Amp Lee doesn't keep his feet moving. One thing about Watters, he will explode through things; Amp Lee, when he starts to get hit, stops his feet. That's what great running backs do: They never stop their feet. They always have that forward lean. They always have that head up. They always keep those feet moving and they're trying to find soft spots and not have square contacts. By keeping those feet going, guys are gonna bounce off you, and you have a chance to pick up more yards. –*49ers at Lions (12/19/93)*

On Bears RB Raymont Harris: He has a good feel, like Emmitt Smith. I'm not saying that Raymont Harris is Emmitt Smith [but they both excel at] what you call *pick-a-hole* – where you hand them the ball and they start one direction and they just pick a hole anywhere around the line of scrimmage. Some guys are slashers or straight-ahead guys. Lewis Tillman, for example, is a slasher. He's gonna go in one direction. Some guys are pick-a-hole guys. Harris is a pick-a-hole guy. –*NFC Wildcard, Bears at Vikings (1/1/95)*

On Cowboys RB Emmitt Smith gaining a first down on third-and-one: That's why Emmitt Smith is so good: It's short yardage. You know that he is gonna get the ball. Everyone is keying on him. All you have to do is follow [FB] Moose Johnston because he's gonna lead him, and he still gets the first down. There's nothing you can do about it. To me, *that's* greatness. –*Cowboys at Chargers (10/15/95)*

On Lions RB Barry Sanders, after a 50-yard scoring run: He said the reason he never celebrates or shows any emotion is because there's more work to be done. He said, if it was ever the last play of the game in the Super Bowl, maybe he would. But until then he doesn't see any reason to celebrate until all your work is done. –*Vikings at Lions (11/23/95)*

On Giants RB Rodney Hampton: [Bears LB] Joe Cain said during the week that Rodney Hampton's fat. He called him a "fat back." He said he's hard to tackle sometimes. You always want to look at a guy's midsection when you're making a tackle; you always watch his belt. Cain said that Hampton's so fat that when he moves he makes you seasick. –*Bears at Giants (11/26/95)*

On Cowboys tailback Emmitt Smith's durability: We were talking to [Redskins RB] Terry Allen about Emmitt Smith. He said, "Everyone says that he's a workhorse, that they run him too much and they're gonna burn him out. But that's not going to happen because the big guys don't usually tackle him. His line is so good that it gets him past the defensive line and linebackers. If you watch Emmitt Smith, he is usually being tackled by defensive backs." –*Redskins at Cowboys (12/3/95)*

On Bears RB Rashaan Salaam's fumbling affecting his performance: Fumbling sometimes takes away the aggressiveness from your running because you're not balanced well. You become so conscious of holding onto the ball that you can't run. You're just running and you have no balance and you don't stride out or anything. He looked like he was more worried about holding onto that ball and not fumbling or being stripped than he was making yards on that play. –*Eagles at Bears (12/24/95)*

On Eagles RB Ricky Waters' poor blocking, which led to a sack: Here's Lee Woodall coming from the left side, and Ricky Waters is supposed to block him. That was a poor, poor, poor blocking effort by Ricky Waters. That's terrible. That stinks. You've got to be able to run the ball, you've got to be able to catch the ball. But the other thing you have to do as a running back is be able to pass protect. –*NFC Wildcard, Eagles at 49ers (12/29/96)*

On a scoring run by Patriots RB Curtis Martin: Curtis Martin was really something once he hit that hole. This guy has moves upon moves. He has moves in the backfield. He has moves in the hole. He has strength, and he has moves when he gets in the open field. He says all he sees is opposite color; he runs *away* from opposite color. –*Super Bowl XXXI, Patriots vs. Packers (1/26/97)*

On Lions tailback Barry Sanders: Barry Sanders will put you in a highlight film if you are a defensive player, but it won't be your highlight. –*Giants at Lions (10/19/97)*

On using "great" to describe Lions RB Barry Sanders: I think that's the one time you have freedom of use of the word. –*Bears at Lions (11/27/97)*

More on Barry Sanders: I think when you say pure runner – *pure running of the football* – he's the best there is. I've never seen a better one. –*Bears at Lions (11/27/97)*

On Buccaneers 5-9 tailback Warrick Dunn: Everyone thinks he's a little back. When you see all these plays he's running, all these lead plays and inside draw things, all those cuts he's making, you realize that he's not a little back. His calves look like they have a cramp in them all the time. His calves are always in a bulge. They never relax. They always look like they're making a Popeye muscle all the time. –*NFC Wildcard, Lions at Buccaneers (12/28/97)*

On Broncos RB Terrell Davis: If you say how did the Denver Broncos get to be world champions, I say it's because of that guy. In the second half of that Super Bowl against the Green Bay Packers, after he had those migraine headaches, that was one of the greatest efforts I've ever seen in football. He had to take medication when he had the migraines. Then he came back and they gave [Green Bay] a big dose of Terrell Davis in the second half and the Packers just couldn't stop him. –*Cowboys at Broncos (9/13/98)*

On Packers RB Travis Jervey's inside running: Do you get the feeling that every time Travis Jervey runs in there, it's like he's running into a wall? That he doesn't have any feel at all? A couple years ago [Packers coach] Mike Holmgren was telling us about Travis Jervey. They had this drill with a seven-man sled, where the backs run inside then they bounce outside the sled. Jervey ran right into the sled. –*49ers at Packers (11/1/98)*

On Vikings fullback Leroy Hoard: Leroy Hoard said the other day, "If you need a yard, I'll get you three; if you need five yards, I'll get you three." –*Vikings at Cowboys (11/26/98)*

On Rams tailback Marshall Faulk: He has great speed and quickness and vision and all that stuff. He was saying that he doesn't have to look where he's going, so defensive guys can't key his eyes.... Remember as a kid, when you'd run into a wall or something, and someone would always yell, "Look where you're going?" Probably, in his life, no one ever yelled at Marshall Faulk, "Hey, look where you're going!" But then he learned to go where *you're* not looking. –*NFC Playoffs, Vikings at Rams (1/16/00)*

On "little" Buccaneers RB Warrick Dunn: Yesterday we were talking to him and asked him, "How do you not get hurt?" It's a stupid question because he's been playing so long "little." I mean, he was little in high school, little in college, little in the pros as a number one draft choice. He says when he goes down, he just gets in a fetal position...After the play's over, you're not gonna get any more of him than that. He never gets hit squarely. –*NFC Wildcard, Buccaneers at Eagles (12/31/00)*

On a short reception by Rams FB James Hodgins: James Hodgins is a *big* fullback. By big, I mean a guy who weighs 270 pounds. His nickname's

"Meat." I think most fullbacks should be nicknamed "Meat." If you're a fullback and you're gonna be out in the middle of the field, and you're gonna run patterns like that, you have to be "Meat." Now, what do you think [Pats cornerback] Ty Law is thinking when he sees 270 pounds of "Meat" coming at him? *Tackle him low. –Super Bowl XXXVI, Rams vs. Patriots (2/3/02)*

On Rams tailback Marshall Faulk's awareness as a runner: He said sometimes he'll look at the third or fourth tackler and just assume that the first guy was gonna miss anyway... He has patience. He's not running full speed, but he's looking. He has the vision to look beyond [the first tackler]. He said he sees colors flash in front of him then runs away from flashing colors. *–Rams at Eagles (9/9/01)*

On Rams RB Marshall Faulk being healthy: We were talking to Marshall Faulk last night, and we said, "Are you healthy?" He said, "Let me tell you something about being healthy. The last time I was healthy was before the Houston Oiler game in 1994." It was his first game. *–Rams at Eagles (9/9/01)*

On the importance of blocking: If you're gonna be a running back in this league, obviously you're gonna have to be able to run the ball and be able to catch it. But if you can't block, you can't play because they'll take advantage of you. [The defense] will *make* you block or protect. *–Colts at Buccaneers (10/6/03)*

On Broncos tailback Clinton Portis: One of the things Bill Belichick said about Clinton Portis that I really don't agree with is that he's not a power runner, that he's not powerful. I believe he *is* powerful. Because when he gets low, he gets lower than you do. And if his power is underneath your power, he is going to be more powerful than you. And he can get himself in those positions where I feel he is *very* powerful. *–Patriots at Broncos (11/3/03)*

On Colts tailback Edgerrin James: You know what I like about Edgerrin James? When he's healthy, he has about *three* cuts. Usually a running back will take a cut then take it to the hole. Or take a cut then cut it back. Edgerrin James will take it playside, backside, then *back* to playside. He's the only back I know that does that on a regular basis. *–Colts at Patriots 9/9/04*

Recalling Emmitt Smith's heroic performance versus the Giants in 1993: There was only one time, since I've been a broadcaster, that I went into a locker room after a game to congratulate a player. It was to Emmitt Smith on that day. They were putting ice all over his body. He had IVs in both arms. He doesn't remember anything. But I said, "This is one of the greatest performances that I've ever seen in my life." *–Redskins at Cowboys (9/19/05)*

Chapter 4: RECEIVERS & ENDS

Madden: "The great ones like Jerry Rice have no fear going over the middle."

On Saints WR Wes Chandler leaving game with a groin pull: I saw when he was thrown to the turf. It looked like he did the splits. That's what usually happens on that type of action; you get the groin pull. There's no good injury in football, but a groin is a lot better injury for Wes Chandler than a knee would be. –*Saints at 49ers, Madden's first CBS telecast (9/23/79)*

On Eagles receiver Harold Carmichael: He told me once, "You know, just because I'm 6-foot-7 doesn't mean they can throw it 8-foot-2. I don't like it when they do because I don't like to be up there exposed." –*Eagles at Giants (9/6/81)*

On height at the tight end position: The closer you get to the goal line, the more important a big tight end is because you can see him down there. –*Eagles at Giants (9/6/81)*

On why his Raider teams never used a wide-receiver option pass: We used to have a tough time throwing those things when they wore Stickum. We used to practice that all week. Then we'd try to do it in the game and couldn't throw it because they had Stickum on. –*Cowboys at 49ers (10/11/81)*

On Packers' misuse of offensive firepower: On that last play, what was funny was they had two great wide receivers, James Lofton and John Jefferson – high priced, pay 'em a lot of money – on the left side. And they were both blockers for Harlan Huckleby. Weird. –*Giants at Packers (11/8/81)*

On the career stats of Eagles WR Harold Carmichael: Look at all those yards he's gained. I haven't gotten that many numbers on a pinball machine. –*Giants at Eagles (11/22/81)*

On a botched Cowboys' wide receiver screen play: One thing that Tony Hill should know by now is that against this Eagle defense – it's always been a swarming defense – if you get that ball, you'd better not dance with it. Get it and take it straight up the field. Tony Hill did a little dance out there, and a whole bunch of those green shirts came out and said hello. –*Eagles at Cowboys (12/13/81)*

On Cowboys receiver Butch Johnson: Butch Johnson has the strongest hands of any receiver I've ever seen. He has big hands. He's not a big man, but when you shake hands with him, he has hands like a tackle. –*Eagles at Cowboys (12/13/81)*

On famed hurdler Renaldo Nehemiah joining 49ers as a receiver: There was a lot of talk about Nehemiah getting hit. I think it's more than that. Everything he has done has been individual – running track in a lane, jumping a hurdle. Now there are 22 men out there. To him, it has to look like the Los Angeles Freeway. It's not a matter of getting hit. He's a fine athlete; he'll be able to handle that. It's being able to make all the adjustments and find the seams. *Is it zone or man?* –*Raiders at 49ers (8/14/82)*

On Giants WR Ernest Gray avoiding tackles by going out of bounds: MADDEN: That was pretty smart. He catches a short pass, starts inside and sees all those white jerseys and says *Whoa! I don't want to go in there! Let me go back where there's no guys!* He got out of bounds. That's that old psychology test, where if the rat goes in and turns left, he gets the cheese; if he turns right they hit him over the head with something. They go in after the cheese; then they see all those jerseys and go to the sideline.

SUMMERALL: Maybe Gray saw some cheese out of bounds. –*Rams at Giants (9/4/83)*

On Rams tight end Mike Barber: MADDEN: You know how on defense they always have a big tackle hanging around the line of scrimmage? He handles the draw and the screen. Chews tobacco and stuff. On offense they have the same type of guy. The other guys go deep, but some guy hangs around the line of scrimmage for that drop-off. That's the kind of guy Barber is. He doesn't go deep. He kinda hangs around. When everything's covered deep, they give him the ball.

SUMMERALL: Another one of those guys with a pickup truck.

MADDEN: Yep. Pickup truck. Shotgun. Willie Nelson for President. –*Rams at Jets (9/25/83)*

On Cowboys RB Timmy Newsome diving for a deep pass: You know what he did wrong? He left his feet. I always teach receivers – don't dive for the ball. Run through it. The greatest I ever had at that was Fred Biletnikoff. He would never leave his feet. He would run through everything. It looked like Newsome stopped to dive, and that's where you lose the speed. –*Eagles at Cowboys (10/16/83)*

On Eagles TE Vyto Kab dropping a pass: There's a guy that has a tough time against the Cowboys. In the first game he didn't catch a pass. He hasn't caught a pass in this game. He's had two thrown to him and dropped them both. So, he's 0-for-Cowboys. –*Cowboys at Eagles (11/6/83)*

On a key block thrown by Cowboys WR Butch Johnson: Did you see who it was on? It was on a defensive tackle – Stafford Mays. Butch Johnson, a wide receiver, came in motion and blocked the defensive tackle. I never had a wide receiver who would do that. If I ever said, "Hey Fred Biletnikoff or Cliff Branch, why don't you go in there and block that defensive tackle? He weighs about 280." They'd look and say, "Huh? You do it!" –*Cardinals at Cowboys (11/24/83)*

On downfield blocking: On any big play by a running back, there has to be a block by a wide receiver. –*Cardinals at Cowboys (11/24/83)*

On Raiders WR Cliff Branch beating a zone defense for a long gain: You just can't *run* a pass pattern against a zone; you feel it. Watch Cliff Branch. He's gonna go in. He feels where all those guys are. He situates himself right in the middle of four of them, works back a little, and gets the ball. You don't run all out against a zone; you feel for holes in it. –*Giants at Raiders (11/27/83)*

On Raiders WR Cliff Branch: I remember when Cliff Branch was a rookie. The first time he scored a touchdown, he spiked the ball. I said, "Don't ever do that again, Cliff! You're too small. Don't cause attention. Don't bring attention to you." Since that time, he's never spiked the football in the endzone. He always hands it to the official. –*Super Bowl XVIII, Redskins vs. Raiders (1/22/84)*

On Falcons tight end Arthur Cox: They say he's one of the strongest men on the Atlanta Falcon team, but [coach] Dan Henning said, "That's really not what you need in a tight end. Strength is usually not a weakness of a person. But sometimes strength *can* be someone's weakness when they can't do a lot of moving." –*Falcons at Rams (10/7/84)*

On poor technique of Jets WR Bobby Humphrey: Watch Humphrey here. He's just gonna run up and run a little hook pattern. One thing he's doing is catching the ball too close into his body. That one went right through his hands, hit his shoulder pads, hit his facemask, then bounced back into his hands. That's going through a lot of stuff to only pick up nine yards. –*Giants at Jets (12/2/84)*

On Cardinals WR Roy Green: Roy Green is an amazing guy. He's one of the few guys who can run *through* a zone. Everyone says you can't get deep on a zone, that you can't *throw* deep against a zone. Well, it all depends on who's throwing and who's running and who's catching. Because this guy *can*. They have a safety sitting back there, and he just runs right by him. –*Cardinals at Redskins (12/16/84)*

On Raiders tight end Dave Casper: When he used to catch the ball in the open field...he loved to get his shoulders square, turn up, and try to find a defensive back who'd jump on him. Then he would measure how far he gave the guy a ride. He had records for stuff like that. –*NFC Wildcard, Giants at Rams (12/23/84)*

On Giants throwing deep early in the game: That's the type of play that, even though Bobby Johnson dropped it, proved a number of things. It proved that there's good pass protection that's gonna give [QB] Phil Simms time. And it told the Eagles *You'd better watch out; we're gonna go deep with some speed*. Those things, even though they don't get you touchdowns, get you a heckuva lot that you can use and work on later. –*Eagles at Giants (9/8/85)*

On Eagles tight end Vyto Kab: His name originally was Kabashinski. If he goes by Kabashinski, then he has to play nose tackle. *Hey, Vyto Kabashinski! Get in there in the middle!* Now that it's Kab, he can be a nice tight end on the outside, that kinda thing. –*Eagles at Giants (9/8/85)*

On Giants rookie TE Mark Bavaro: Bavaro's an interesting guy. He came to camp and didn't know anyone. No one knew him. This is the ninth game of the regular season and he's still the same way. No one knows him. Doesn't talk to anyone. Doesn't talk to players, coaches. They're thinking *Is that guy weird or is he just quiet?* –*Buccaneers at Giants (11/3/85)*

On Giants WR Lionel Manuel losing a first down by retreating: I used to always tell my receivers, "I like you to try, I like you to break [tackles], but don't ever get a first down and then lose it because you're trying to make more. If you get a first down, let 'em move the chains. We'll take that. But don't start jumping and jump back and lose the first down! –*Buccaneers at Giants (11/3/85)*

On tackling Giants TE Mark Bavaro: [Safety] Stacy Toran knows about Mark Bavaro…They were teammates at Notre Dame, so Toran knows that when you get Bavaro you better hold on until you get some help. It's gonna take a couple of 'em to get that guy down. I've never seen tacklers bounce off a receiver as much as I've seen off this guy. This guy leads the league in tacklers that have bounced off his body. –*Giants at Raiders (9/21/86)*

On the skill of catching deep passes: When you run fast, your eyes bounce up and down. Sometimes it's tough to adjust to that long pass. It takes time to learn how to do that, to run fast and not bounce your eyes. I never had that problem, but Cliff Branch had that problem, when he'd run so fast he couldn't see something. –*Giants at Raiders (9/21/86)*

On Giants TE Mark Bavaro: Every coach you ask, "Who's the best tight end?" they say *this* guy, Mark Bavaro. I don't know that *Bavaro* thinks that. He's one of the shyest professional football players I've ever met. He never says a word. He doesn't talk to anyone. Doesn't talk to his teammates. Doesn't talk to his coaches. Doesn't talk to the opponents. He just goes and plays football. Bill Parcells was telling us he has a big bowl. He pours a box of cereal, a quart of milk, and some bananas in it. And he just walks around with a ladle eating this cereal. And lifting weights. –*NFC Championship Game, Redskins at Giants (1/11/87)*

On Steelers WR John Stallworth: When the Steelers were winning those Super Bowls – of course, they had Lynn Swann on the other side – I always thought the most underrated player and maybe the best of the receivers was this guy here, John Stallworth. –*Giants at Steelers (9/5/87)*

On Giants TE Mark Bavaro resembling tennis player Slobodan Živojinović: That's what Pat Summerall said today. Except Bavaro is a little bigger. He's got some more meat on his bones. Plus "Živojinović" would have to be a nose tackle. –*Giants at Steelers (9/5/87)*

On "refocused" Giants WR Lionel Manual: Bill Parcells was saying this guy is a *different* guy. He's in better shape. He's concentrating more. He's better than he ever was. In fact, he's married now and he's in a bowling league. When you get a guy who's married and in a bowling league, you've got a settled-down wide receiver. He probably has a station wagon and a lawn mower. I always said, when I was coaching, that the toughest group to coach and handle and get along with and motivate were the single players. They were always the toughest guys. Those married guys, when practice is over, they had a place to go. They had to go home. Single? You had no idea where those guys were going. –*49ers at Giants (9/11/88)*

On short passes going for long yardage: That's the thing that makes big plays out of average plays – explosive guys when they catch it, and other wide receivers in front making a block. –*Saints at Redskins (11/6/88)*

After a dropped pass by Giants TE Howard Cross: Cross looks like a tight end who's a good blocker but can't catch. It's like a blind date who has a nice personality. –*Giants at Eagles (10/8/89)*

On Bears TE Cap Boso protesting the spot of the ball: Boso is helping the official spot the ball. He's saying, "Here! Right here!" The official didn't pay any attention to ol' Boso. He put the ball back where he wanted to. You walk around with B-O-S-O on your back and they aren't going to listen to you much. –*Bears at Redskins (11/26/89)*

On Dolphins WR Paul Warfield: Bob Griese would throw it to him, and he ran slants or post patterns better than anyone I ever saw play the game. –*Rams at 49ers (9/22/91)*

On 49ers WR John Taylor's willingness to go over the middle: All the great ones do it; the average ones don't go inside with the same enthusiasm. –*Rams at 49ers (9/22/91)*

On 49ers WR Jerry Rice: One of the best things about Jerry Rice is he comes out of a break quickly. He can run fast, but a lot of guys can run fast. But he doesn't lose speed when he slows down to make a break. –*49ers at Giants (9/6/92)*

On free agent WR Tom Waddle beating All-Pro CB Deion Sanders: Every time I've seen this guy play, every time we've done a Bear game, Tom Waddle has had a big game…He shouldn't be running by guys like Deion Sanders. He shouldn't be running a corner pattern in the endzone and not have Deion Sanders right on him. You say, "That can't be done. You can't do that!" Oh yeah? Take a look. He just did it. –*Falcons at Bears (9/27/92)*

On ability of Eagles WR Fred Barnett: Fred Barnett is one of the few guys in the NFL who can run through double coverage. There can be double coverage, and [Barnett] can still beat it. The other thing he can do is run through a zone. Everyone says you can't throw deep against a zone. If there's a safety sitting in the middle, you can't throw deep. *Normally* you can't. But Fred Barnett can run through it and past it… If you have Barnett out there, I think you can *throw it* into double coverage. I think you can *throw it* through a zone. –*Eagles at Redskins (10/18/92)*

On unique makeup of Broncos tight end Shannon Sharpe: He was a wide receiver. Then they moved him to H-back, so they list him as a tight end. Then the Broncos got all these telephone calls from these fantasy league players. *Is Shannon Sharpe a receiver or a tight end?* In truth, he's listed as a tight end. But he's one of those in-between guys, half wide receiver and half tight end. –*Cowboys at Broncos (12/6/92)*

On Cowboys WR Michael Irvin: We were talking to Troy Aikman last night, and we said, "When do you consider a guy to be open?" He said, "When it's Michael Irvin one on one. Any time I get single coverage, I'm going to him. He's open." –*Cowboys at Dolphins (10/27/96)*

On Cowboys WR Anthony Miller's reputation of being fast: We saw Anthony Miller on that play before *trying* to beat [CB] Darnell. Walker. They always say Anthony Miller has good speed, but I've never seen it in a game. I have never seen Anthony Miller use his speed to beat *anyone* deep in a game. That's the thing the Cowboys were counting on today: If they're gonna double Michael Irvin, then Anthony Miller is gonna have to come up and make big plays. They say he has great speed, but I've never seen him separate or outrun anyone in a game. –*Cowboys at 49ers (11/2/97)*

On good hands: Any time you hear a ball hit hands, those are bad hands. You can hear *good* hands by not hearing them. Any time you hear *SLAP!* those are bad hands. –*Panthers at Broncos (11/9/97)*

On the Vikings' lightning-fast scoring drives: When you have Randall Cunningham chucking the ball down the field like that, and you have Randy Moss running under it, it's not gonna take a lot of time unless you have like a 500-yard field. When they throw it *50* yards, that's gonna be touchdowns. – *Vikings at Cowboys (11/26/98)*

On defending WR Randy Moss: It's tough when you know a guy can outjump you, and that same guy can also outrun you. Then you'd better grab ahold of anything you can. –*Vikings at Cowboys (11/26/98)*

On blocking: For wide receivers, ninety percent of blocking is wanting-to. –*Cowboys at Eagles (10/10/99)*

On explosiveness of Vikings WR Randy Moss: I would say you throw two deep passes a quarter to him. That would be eight per game. If you did that, you're going to have four or five big plays. You're either gonna get a touchdown or have a pass interference...To me, this guy is the most dangerous player in all of football. –*NFC Wildcard, Cowboys at Vikings (1/9/00)*

On the speed of the Rams receiving corps: Everyone is surprised by the Rams' speed all the time. In fact, what Bill Belichick did [to prepare] his defense was to have his scout receivers start three yards offsides. They started three yards up the field before the ball was snapped, just to give the feeling of how quickly these [Rams] receivers get up the field on you. –*Super Bowl XXXVI, Rams vs. Patriots (2/3/02)*

On selfishness at the WR position: If there's a selfish position in the NFL, it's the wide receiver position. It's not the quarterback position anymore; it's not the running back anymore. It's the wide receiver. I think sometimes they get carried away with their numbers and worry about those things more than they do winning the game. That's wrong. –*Vikings at Colts (11/8/04)*

Chapter 5: OFFENSIVE LINE

Chicago Bears center Jay Hilgenberg in combat with the Bengals.

On offensive linemen: The only time they get their name mentioned is when they hold. –*Lions at Chiefs (10/26/80)*

On Falcons tackle Warren Bryant being flagged for holding: Warren Bryant wore those red gloves; that's one way you get caught. Listen up, Warren, you don't wear red because if that red glove gets on a white jersey, the official can see it. If you taped those red gloves *white*, then when you get your hand up they can't see it. But the official saw that red glove on the white jersey. –*Falcons at Oilers (11/29/81)*

On Broncos Claudie Minor moving from right tackle to left tackle: It's tough because everything that was inside is now outside, and everything that was outside is now inside.... Everything that was offside is now onside, and everything that was onside is offside. –*49ers at Broncos (9/19/82)*

On the '82 Redskins offensive line: You know what they call the offensive line of the Redskins? Their nickname is "Hogs." I like that kinda talk – Hogs! But they ought to be playing in grass, though, in mud. With stuff hanging off their facemask and out of their nose and mud on their pants. Here on the artificial turf, it's hard for a Hog to be a Hog. –*Redskins at Giants (11/21/82)*

On Redskins' 6-7, 305-lb tackle Joe Jacoby: How'd you like to be a linebacker and you're sitting in the hole and see this guy coming at you? Look at the size of that guy. I'll tell ya, *he* never ate cottage cheese. –*Redskins at Giants (11/13/83)*

On the Raiders drafting tackle Henry Lawrence in 1974: We saw him in the Senior Bowl. Ed "Too Tall" Jones of the Dallas Cowboys was the number one player chosen that year. Henry Lawrence was on Jones' team. We're watching them practice and Henry was blocking "Too Tall." I said, "If 'Too Tall' is the best guy in the draft, and this guy's *blocking* him, maybe we ought to take *him*." That's how we drafted Henry Lawrence number one that year. –*Giants at Raiders (11/27/83)*

On a group of Redskins fans inside Texas stadium: You love to see the Hogs have some supporters. They ought to! You see [guard] Russ Grimm there? He just blew Randy White right off the line of scrimmage. These guys only know one way to play. You get down there and *WHOMP!* Watch the left guard on Randy White – *BOOM!* Just head in there, drive those legs, knock 'em right off the line of scrimmage. Fourth quarter, ahead by 21 points? They don't care. Just get down and grunt and play. That's why the Redskins win. –*Redskins at Cowboys (12/11/83)*

On an offsides flag on Raiders DE Lyle Alzado: It looks like [tackle] Joe Jacoby was tipping a little and Alzado just took off. When you're like Jacoby and you're over 300 pounds and you're starting to tip, it could register on one of those scales. –*Super Bowl XVIII, Redskins vs. Raiders (1/22/84)*

On inexperienced Bears guard Mark Bortz facing All-Pro tackle Randy White: Bortz was a defensive player originally. He couldn't make it, so they moved him to offense. Now he's starting. Mike Ditka said yesterday, "The good thing about Bortz having to block Randy White is he's naïve. He doesn't know. He's never heard of him. He doesn't know what he's in for." –*Cowboys at Bears (9/30/84)*

On the building blocks of a winning team: They always talk about *How do you start a team?* I've always said offensive line. Not quarterback. Not the wide receivers. Not the defensive ends. You start with the offensive line because if you don't have those guys, if they can't block, everything else goes academic. You can't do anything else. –*Eagles at Giants (9/8/85)*

After a holding call on Cowboys tackle Phil Pozderac: I remember when Phil Pozderac just started. Tom Landry said, "You'd love this guy. He knows how to hold the way those Raiders do." –*Cowboys at Redskins (11/10/85)*

On former Steelers guard Steve Courson, now on the Buccaneers: Remember him? He was a lot bigger. He lost about 25 pounds. He used to be on steroids. He's one of those steroid guys who got up where he could bench press 550 pounds, and the steroids darned-near killed him. He came into a mini-camp and his standing heart-rate was 168 beats a minute. He got off the steroids, lost the weight, and he doesn't have the same strength now. But you don't *need* it! You have to be able to move! You need agility! You don't need [steroids]. Now he can move his neck from right to left. He can pick his arms up. He can comb his hair. –*Buccaneers at Giants (11/3/85)*

On a penalty against Eagles guard Ken Reaves: Those poor offensive linemen. The guy blocks all day. He jumps offsides once and *BOOM!* The referee tells everyone, "Number 66 jumped offsides." The ref will never say, "Hey, number 66 made a heckuva block. Did you see it?" –*Eagles at Redskins (9/7/86)*

On the Redskins' goal line formation: They got their big old Heavy Jumbo offense in there. You take out the quarterback, because he's not gonna block anyone. The running back is George Rogers, who's gonna carry the ball. This group weighs 2,427 pounds! They average 270-pounds a guy. That's a *Heavy* Jumbo. You've got Jumbo's, your light and medium. This is the ol' *Heavy* Jumbo. They ought to just push the whole thing back into the endzone. –*Redskins at Broncos (12/13/86)*

On lineage of Bears center Jay Hilgenberg: That guy's whole family played center. They never played "catch" in their life *facing* each other. They used to be in the backyard, and all they'd see is the backsides going all the time. Shirts hanging out, stuff like that. –*NFC Championship Game, Rams at Bears (1/12/86)*

On injured Cowboys guard Nate Newton limping to the locker room: That's what's different with offensive linemen – when they go in [for treatment], no one even helps them. Backs, receivers, quarterbacks, they have like eight guys [helping them]. To some of these linemen they say, "Well, you just go in on your own." If that guy was a quarterback, there'd be guys holding stuff, carrying his helmet, helping him. –*Cowboys at Giants (9/20/87)*

On injured Bears tackle Jimbo Covert: He's up here in the Bears coaching booth. I asked him what he was doing. He said he was "watching for Raiders blitzes." I said, "How're they doing?" He said, "I don't know." That's a tackle for ya. You don't put a tackle up there [to watch for blitzes]! What's *he* know? He knows where the hot dogs are. He doesn't know about blitzes. He doesn't know where the safeties are. –*Bears at Raiders (12/27/87)*

On Covert's backup, tackle John Wojciechowski: The guy who's taken his place, Wojciechowski, is doing a pretty good job. They haven't really run to his side, but he's done a pretty good job of pass protection. He also does a pretty good job of holding that name up on his back. That's 13 letters in that name, and that's an NFL record – *Most Letters on a Back in the NFL*. They start all the way under his armpit and go all the way to the other armpit. – *Bears at Raiders (12/27/87)*

On the importance of the offensive line: Everything starts in the line. You can have all these plays and designs but if you don't get the thing blocked, nothing means anything. –*NFC Wildcard, Vikings at Saints (1/3/88)*

On Falcons tackle Bill Fralic being a tough guy: We had him a couple of years ago on the All-Madden team. In WrestleMania II, he got in there and he was one of the last guys thrown out of the ring. He said his *dad* was a tough guy. His dad was a big guy, like 6-3, 250. He had a sign at his house. It said, "Don't worry about the dog. Beware of the owner." –*Giants at Falcons (10/23/88)*

On short-yardage rushing touchdowns: Offensive linemen love running touchdowns. When you can get your running back in there and plow into the endzone, the most excited guys are those offensive linemen. *That's what they live for!* –*NFC Playoffs, Vikings at 49ers (1/1/89)*

On 49ers tackle Bruce Collie: He just learned to fly an airplane, and he flew down to San Francisco from training camp in Rocklin. (Coach) George Seifert said that was okay. But listen who he took! He took Joe Montana and Steve Young with him. He flew them down to San Francisco then back up to Rocklin, which is about one hundred miles! Then Seifert gave him a rule: You can't take both of them at the same time! –*Broncos at 49ers (8/19/89)*

On the talent levels of an offensive line: Of your offensive linemen, usually your tackles are your best pass protectors; the guards are the next-best pass protectors, and the center is the least of the pass protectors and talent. –*Giants at Eagles (10/8/89)*

On Cowboys 320-lb guard Nate Newton: You ever notice how a heavy guy will always pull up his pants? Watch Nate Newton. He made a good block that time on Jerome Brown. Then they'll always pull up their pants. And your shirt tail is always hanging out. When you're a fat guy, you always dream of the day your shirt tail won't hang out...It's block, block, block, and then you pull up your pants. –*Eagles at Cowboys (11/23/89)*

On 49ers tackle Bubba Paris: When Bubba Paris is in there, they like to run behind him. They don't pull him much. That's because, although they list him at 299, Bubba is closer to 399 than 299. He's not [quite] 399. He'll get mad when I say that, but he's closer to 399 than 299! –*Super Bowl XXIV, 49ers vs. Broncos (1/28/90)*

On understated weight of Cowboys guard Jeff Zimmerman: He has his own zip code, this guy. He gets bigger as he goes down (from head to toe). He's wearing a flak jacket, and as he goes down he just keeps getting bigger. I bet he's 335, 340, 350. How'd you like to be a turkey, just hanging around and knowing he's coming home after the game? –*Redskins at Cowboys (11/22/90)*

On massive 49ers tackle Bubba Paris being penalized for lining up offside: They're saying that Bubba is lined up off the ball. He's back too far; he's in the backfield. Which *he is*. But when you weigh 350-pounds, some of you is gonna be on the line of scrimmage, and the other of ya is gonna be in the backfield! You can't penalize a man for *that*! –*Saints at 49ers (12/23/90)*

On an injury suffered by Giants LT Jumbo Elliott: MADDEN: I think the Giants slumped a little when they lost Jumbo Elliott. He had a broken leg for a while. Then when he came back, he gave them that big guy they need on that offensive line, that guy to kinda anchor, to kinda hang everyone else on.

SUMMERALL: When he had that broken leg, he wouldn't talk about it...You'd ask him, "How are you?" *I'm fine.* "Why aren't you playing?" *I'm fine.*

MADDEN: They say it's non-weight bearing, but when you're *that* big? I mean, that guy fills out that stuff. He's well over 300 pounds. *Everything* is weight bearing. –*NFC Playoffs, Bears at Giants (1/13/91)*

On Redskins tackle Joe Jacoby: When [Lions DT] Jerry Ball was talking about mean guys, he said, "Joe Jacoby is a *mean* guy." I said, "What do you mean? What's a mean guy?" He said, "I'll tell you what a mean guy is. A mean guy is a guy that can get mad and then *do* something about it." There aren't a lot of offensive linemen that you'd call "mean guys." But for a guy like Jerry Ball, out of the blue, to say Joe Jacoby is a mean guy, that's a compliment. –*Lions at Redskins (9/20/92)*

On Redskins rookie center Matt Elliott: There's the ol' Lowsman! He was the last player taken in the NFL draft. The Redskins have the Heisman (Desmond Howard) and the Lowsman. –*Lions at Redskins (9/20/92)*

On Chiefs offensive line faking a run play: The line blows out, and they make noises, the way big guys make noises in the trench. They all go,

"Brrruhhh! Brrruhhh!" to make you really believe that it's a run. Then [the defense comes up and they throw it deep]. –*Redskins at Chiefs (11/15/92)*

On Cowboys offensive tackle Erik Williams: I was talking about the right tackle, Erik Williams, as being one of the real good ones. He's so big and so strong. Watch his arms come up, and he gets his hands on [DE Eric] Dorsey. From that point on, you don't have a chance. When a guy is that big and strong, and his arms are that long, there's no way you're gonna go through him. And you can't go around him. –*Giants at Cowboys (11/26/92)*

On replay of Cowboys lineman Kevin Gogan being tackle-eligible: He's wide open there in the endzone. Troy Aikman didn't see him. Heck, he didn't even look for him. *I'm open! I got it! I'm uncovered! I got a step on my guy!* Gogan is over there saying, "I don't know what else I have to do. I was wide open. I gave them my best moves. What more do you want from me? What's a guy have to do to catch a ball in this league?" Aikman looks bored. He's not even listening. Gogan is telling him how open he is. Aikman hears that from everyone. He doesn't expect it from some big ol' backup tackle. –*Cowboys at Broncos (12/6/92)*

On pass blocking: The toughest pass protection is the side the quarterback's throwing to. Because you not only have to block your man, you also have to create a passing lane. –*NFC Playoffs, Redskins at 49ers (1/9/93)*

On Cowboys 330-lb guard Nate Newton playing at muddy Candlestick Park: I was talking to Nate yesterday on the field. He was saying, "One thing about being a heavy guy is you don't have to worry about your footing. Because when you put these feet in the ground, with that weight on top of it, those feet are gonna stay in the ground. Those little ol' light guys slip and fall around. But for big ol' guys with a solid base in each sinker, everything kinda sinks right down in on you." –*NFC Championship Game, Cowboys at 49ers (1/17/93)*

On Redskins 6-7 tackle Joe Jacoby: Did you see big Joe Jacoby? Watch him pull. He's gonna start on that left side, he goes to the right, and once he gets it turned up and square, things are gonna go backwards. He's like a bull in a china closet. He blocked about four Eagles. –*Redskins at Eagles (9/19/93)*

On injured Cowboys tackle Mark Tuinei: MADDEN: They probably never talked about Mark Tuinei as much as they have this week. He's been playing here for 12 years. He's one of those guys that protects the back side of Troy Aikman. He's one of those guys that, until he's not there, you don't miss him. Then you say, "Oh, no! Tuinei can't play!"

SUMMERALL: He said before the game, "I'm tired of being called underrated."

MADDEN: It's not that he's underrated as much as this Cowboy team has so many offensive stars. When you take Michael Irvin and Harper and Novacek and Johnston and Emmitt Smith and Troy Aikman and the Pro Bowlers Nate Newton and Erik Williams, by the time you start talking about Tuinei, he comes up about the seventh or eighth or ninth guy! –*Cardinals at Cowboys (10/9/94)*

On Cowboys tackle Erik Williams mauling DE William Fuller in retaliation for a hit on the quarterback: Erik Williams knocked William Fuller down and stood above him and wouldn't let him up. I think that's for the Troy Aikman hit…I think Erik Williams has decided that Fuller isn't going to make any more plays today. He's gonna block him until that whole thing's over. He's gonna take a takedown, then he's gonna get a pin. That was about a five-count pin. Erik Williams had about enough of Fuller today. *You aren't getting near the quarterback anymore.* –*Eagles at Cowboys (10/16/94)*

On Cowboys tackle Erik Williams' aggressive style: That's what you like in an offensive lineman. You don't have to be passive to be an offensive lineman. That's what Erik Williams brings to this Cowboys offensive line – a defensive mentality, a certain toughness that you can take control of a game. –*Eagles at Cowboys (10/16/94)*

On Falcons tackle Mike Kenn: I've always said that Mike Kenn was a picture-perfect pass protector, and you can still say that. 17 years in the league. I think if anyone wanted to know or learn the technique of pass protection, they ought to learn it from Mike Kenn. –*Eagles at Falcons (11/27/94)*

On massive Cowboys guard Derek Kennard being "ineligible downfield": How can a 350-pound guard be downfield on a pass? Maybe that was just *part* of him that got downfield. There's no way he would *intentionally* go downfield. He missed a block, then he got spun around. He's flopping there in space and wandering around. They call *that* "illegal receiver downfield?" That's just a guy that shot air! Derek Kennard goes to hit a guy and completely misses him. He weighs 350 pounds, so that stuff just keeps going. When you miss a guy, the follow-through keeps you going, so you get a little downfield. How can you look at him – from the front or the back – and call him an ineligible receiver? –*Cowboys at Giants (12/24/94)*

On Saints tackle Willie Roaf: Willie Roaf is one of the best offensive tackles in football. You see the way he walks? He always walks up on his toes because he has small calves. Someone told him if you walk on your toes, that will be an exercise for your calves. If you ever watch Willie Roaf walk, he walks real funny. He always exaggerates getting up on his toes to build up his calves. *–49ers at Saints (9/3/95)*

On Cowboys guard Larry Allen: I think this guy is the best offensive lineman in pro football. You watch him on film, and he just dominates everything he does. Run blocking, pass protection – everything he does he dominates. He is so powerful and explosive that he hits guys, and the next thing that hits is the back of their head on the turf. *–Cowboys at Steelers (8/31/97)*

On Cowboys tackle Mark Tuinei: Mark Tuinei was saying to [QB] Troy Aikman, "I heard you're the most accurate quarterback," so he put a Gatorade bottle on top of his head and said, "Let's see you hit this off." Troy said he picked the ball up and threw it and knocked it off. But the amazing part of that story is *not* Troy Aikman. Yes, he can be 25 yards away and knock a bottle off a guy's head. The amazing part is Mark Tuinei. He just put the bottle on top of his head. Troy said he threw it and Tuinei didn't even flinch! Tuinei has to be a guy that doesn't care. If you do *that*, you *have* to not care. *–Cowboys at Steelers (8/31/97)*

On 49ers guard Kevin Gogan getting a workout: Big ol' Gogan has a good sweat going on down there, doesn't he? When you take a guy who's 330 pounds and make a pulling guard out of him, he's gonna gets sweat coming out of places that sweat normally doesn't come out of. He didn't pull a lot with the Dallas Cowboys; they were a straight-ahead team. He didn't pull a lot with the Raiders. Then he comes here and he's pulling all the time. *–Cowboys at 49ers (11/2/97)*

On 49ers guard Kevin Gogan's role as enforcer: You see big, ol' Kevin Gogan get downfield? They say he's a dirty player, but one thing that he does is follow his running back. When his back breaks through, he follows him downfield to make sure nothing happens around the pile, that no one is going to pile on. He's gonna block his guy, make the hole, and now watch 66 come down there. He's checking who's gonna get in on that pile, and *he's* gonna be in on that pile. *–49ers at Packers (11/1/98)*

On a false start penalty by Cowboys tackle Erik Williams: He's just trying to get back on pass protection. The crowd noise is no excuse. Usually when that happens, offensive linemen say, "Oh, the crowd is so noisy and I couldn't hear." Well, when you're at home, you don't have crowd noise on offensive plays. That's just being jumpy. *–Vikings at Cowboys (11/26/98)*

On Bears center Olin Kreutz's unusually low stance: Watch what [QB] Jim Miller has to do with his center Olin Kreutz...Kreutz gets so low that *Miller* has to get low.... That's one of the toughest adjustments Miller ever had to make. The right guard, Chris Vallerial, also gets low. Those two guys get lower than any players I've seen since the famous "Buckets" Goldenberg. He was a guy that used to get *that* low. That's what "bucket" is; that's your bucket. You get your bucket low. *–Packers at Bears (10/7/02)*

On Eagles tackle Jon Runyan: He's a very solid player and a tough guy. One of those guys that if you were gonna take a whole bunch of guys to go do something you didn't know what was gonna be done, you'd take Jon Runyan with you. *–Eagles at 49ers (11/25/02)*

On offensive inconsistency: Any time you have an inconsistent offense, I think it's because of your offensive line. If you don't have a group that has played together for two or three years – or at least a year – your offense cannot be consistent. *–Giants at Buccaneers (11/24/03)*

Chapter 6: DEFENSIVE LINEMEN

Philadelphia Eagles DE Reggie White unloads on the 49ers.

On the run-stopping goal of a nose tackle: That's what a nose man should do – pick up the center, put him in the backfield, and let the runner run into him. *–Eagles at Giants (9/6/81)*

On Eagles DE Dennis Harrison swatting down a pass: Dennis Harrison is 6-foot-8, and when he gets his right arm up he's 7-foot-9. Even though Scott Brunner is 6-foot-5, when he gets his right arm up he's only 7-foot-2. 7-foot-2 can't throw over 7-foot-9. *–Giants at Eagles (11/22/81)*

On the stress of playing nose tackle: Nose tackles get hit from every angle...from straight ahead, from the right side, from the left side, from the back, from the tight end, from everywhere. They ought to pay them a *couple* salaries to play that position. *–Eagles at Cowboys (12/13/81)*

On Redskins DT Dave Butz claiming to weigh 295 pounds*:* When you *admit* to 295, you're always over 300. [Chargers DT] Louie Kelcher admitted to 330. When you admit to 330, you gotta be 350, 360, 370. *–Redskins at Giants (11/21/82)*

On the resurgent play of Cowboys DE Harvey Martin: We know that during the (1982 players) strike, he had that problem where he went bankrupt. That tends to rededicate you. You're broke. That makes you a little hungrier. *–NFC Playoffs, Buccaneers at Cowboys (1/9/83)*

Analyzing a sack by the Buccaneers defense: The player that caused it was Lee Roy Selmon. He comes from the left of the screen, and he's the guy that flushes Danny White. White feels him, he starts to run to the right, and Selmon runs him right into [NT] Dave Logan. Sometimes that first guy has to flush, then the other guys mop up. Flush and mop. –*NFC Playoffs, Buccaneers at Cowboys (1/9/83)*

On Buccaneers nose tackle Dave Logan: Dave Logan kinda hangs around the line of scrimmage pretty well. He says he was born to be a nose tackle. I wonder what it's like to be born a nose tackle. Probably square, solid. Drink a lot of milk. Eat a lot of Pablum. Always have a bottle in your mouth. Probably like to roll around in the dirt, play in the gutters. –*NFC Playoffs, Buccaneers at Cowboys (1/9/83)*

On Redskins DT Dave Butz's shoe size: You talk about a foot! He has size twelve and a half feet. But they're 7E width! He has *seven* E's wide. That's a foundation. –*Giants at Redskins (12/17/83)*

On Redskins DT Daryl Grant: Remember when he first started with the Redskins? On the first day of rookie camp some guy whacked him in the head with a weight and cut his head open. He had to have stitches in his head. He goes out and practices with the stitches in his head, comes back in, leaves his helmet on and continues lifting weights. Joe Gibbs said, "At that moment, I knew he was going to make our team." –*Super Bowl XVIII, Redskins vs. Raiders (1/22/84)*

On Giants NT Jim Burt: In his first year of training camp, he was worried he was gonna get waived. Bill Parcells said Burt was coming to practice and looked tired all the time. He had one of his coaches check it out. Turns out, Burt's roommate had been waived, so he was sleeping underneath his bed in training camp. For two weeks! He thought, "If they come here, they can't find me. They're not gonna cut *me*!" –*Giants at Eagles (10/21/84)*

On Bears DE Dan Hampton: He has the worst-looking hands I've ever seen. He's got those hands, those fingers, that when he makes a fist only about two or three fingers close. A bunch of them just kinda hang up in the air. –*Bears at Cowboys (11/17/85)*

On a rear camera angle of Bears DT William "Refrigerator" Perry: As you look up from the feet, Fridge's thighs are starting to grow together on him a little. See that? There's not much space in there until you get to the knee area. I used to have a player, Art Shell, who I never weighed. The only thing I'd look at was him walking from behind. When the thighs started to grow together, when you didn't see a little gap where you could see some daylight, I'd say, "Art, you gotta lose a little weight." –*Bears at Bengals (9/28/86)*

On escalating weight of Bears DT William "Refrigerator" Perry: This guy's getting bigger. They have those myths and lies, *The check is in the mail* and *Let's have lunch sometime* and *I never go over 55*. Another one of those is *The Fridge weighs 308 pounds*. He's been fined the last two weeks. He's been up to 340. And that's a trained body! Imagine, he's working out every day to get there! –*Bears at Falcon (11/16/86)*

On massive Redskins DT Dave Butz: Last week Giants offensive line coach Fred Hoaglin said that he's got a big old head on him, that it weighs fifty pounds. Butz got upset about that. His teammates called him "Pumpkin Head." So, he went and weighed his own head. He said his head only weighed *twelve* pounds. I think it's more than that. It would be closer to fifty than twelve. –*Redskins at Broncos (12/13/86)*

On Redskins DE Charles Mann leaving the game after tackling QB John Elway: Rule number one in the defensive lineman's playbook is *Never let a quarterback knock you out of the game*. If the quarterback knocks you out of the game, you never get to play again. You can't go dress or shower with the guys. –*Redskins at Broncos (12/13/86)*

On Giants strike-team NT Torin Smith: You talk about a big load, look at *that* guy. He's about 340 pounds. They get two linemen on him and they get him going backwards and going sideways. Then they get him spun around, but they can't get by him. *There's* a guy who throws some shade. You know, they only like the Bubbas – us big guys – at Christmas time for Santa Claus and in summertime for shade. And when they need a defensive lineman for short yardage. Yesterday he said he weighed 308 pounds. I said, "I got a hundred dollars that says you don't." –*Redskins at Giants (10/11/87)*

On underrated Jets NT Joe Klecko: Over the years, Joe Klecko has been one of the best nose tackles probably to ever play this game. –*Eagles at Jets (12/20/87)*

On 49ers NT Michael Carter: When you talk about nose tackles, if you had a prototype and built a statue of one, you'd put some molding around Michael Carter and say, "That's it." He's so short and powerful, and he never gets out of hitting position. He never gets high. Most nose tackles, as they get tired, get higher and higher. You can move 'em out. Carter always stays low. –*49ers at Rams (10/16/88)*

On Bears defensive end Richard Dent's pass-rushing skills: You see why Dent is such a good pass rusher? He's got those long legs. His legs go all the way up to his chest, darn-near. Then he's got those long arms. That's what really makes a good pass rusher – a guy with long arms that can keep offensive blockers away from him, and long legs where you can take long strides in a burst. Probably the other thing that's pretty good is you've got a lot of talent, too...and speed and ability. Just because you've got big ol' long legs and big ol' long arms doesn't necessarily make you a great pass rusher. –*Bears at Redskins (11/13/88)*

On free agent DT Willie Broughton starting for the Cowboys: Jimmy Johnson said, "We aren't really good on defense. We have a guy starting who we didn't contact; he called *us*." When they start calling you, and he's *starting* for you in the league opener, you know where you have to work to improve your team. –*Cowboys at Saints (9/10/89)*

On Eagles front four of Reggie White, Jerome Brown, Clyde Simmons and Mike Pitts: This Eagle defensive line is so big and so powerful. They don't have that quick rush, the way a Minnesota Vikings team does. They have that power rush. They just take all your guys and put 'em in the backfield. Watch how all the blue jerseys are going backwards, and the white jerseys are like an avalanche collapsing on the quarterback. The whole wall just comes down on you. –*Eagles at Giants (12/3/89)*

On NT Jim Burt teaching DT Pierce Holt a move on the sideline: Jim Burt and Pierce Holt are practicing during the game! Burt is coaching Holt how to make a spin move. If a coach saw that, he'd go nuts. Burt is fouling up Holt! He shouldn't do that! You don't want your guys to spin. Holt is blind in his left eye, and now Jim Burt has him spinning! I'll tell ya, [DL coach] John Marshall is gonna go nuts when he hears about that. –*NFC Championship Game, Rams at 49ers (1/14/90)*

On dirty uniforms: When you see a defense with a lot of mud and dirt on their backs, they've had a bad day. A defense should have clean backs after a game. –*NFC Championship Game, Rams at 49ers (1/14/90)*

On Eagles DE Reggie White: There are very few defensive players that can win a game, that can dominate and take over a game. We saw one here last week in Lawrence Taylor, when he's at the top of *his* game. We're seeing another one here – Reggie White. Those are guys that are capable of dominating and winning a game as a defensive player. –*Eagles at Redskins (10/21/90)*

On Redskins DE Charles Mann pulling up on Cowboys QB Troy Aikman: They talk about cheap shot guys and guys taking shots. I've seen Charles Mann pull *off* shots on quarterbacks when he had them more than any other player in the league. If you look at the opposite of a cheap-shot artist, it's this guy right here. He could've ear-holed Aikman, and he let him off the hook. –*Redskins at Cowboys (11/22/90)*

On a battle between Bears DT William "Refrigerator" Perry and Redskins tackle Joe Jacoby, both well over 300 pounds: That's load on load! That's industrial-strength line play. –*Bears at Redskins (12/9/90)*

On the Bears' DT William "Refrigerator" Perry: When you run inside against the Fridge, you aren't gonna get a lot of first downs because most of the bounces go backwards. There aren't many bounces that go forward when you run into 72; they go backwards or sideways or upside down…I wouldn't run it at the Fridge. You don't move that guy. He moves *you* where he wants to move you. –*NFC Playoffs, Bears at Giants (1/13/91)*

On Bears DE Richard Dent destroying a play in the backfield: Richard Dent will wake up a crowd. He plays at about six or seven different levels. Everything's been kinda quiet, and when Richard Dent wants to make a play, you can't block him. I don't care if it's a run or a pass. That time, big [T] Jim Lachey comes up and Dent just throws him off. He grabs [RB] Ernest Byner and throws him down. He's capable of playing like that. He's capable of being unblockable. –*Redskins at Bears (10/6/91)*

On Redskins DE Charles Mann: He was telling us that when he first came to Washington, he weighed 250 pounds. He's now 270. You talk about a guy who's chiseled. When he was a rookie, they told Charles he had to gain weight. So [Cowboys guard] Nate Newton said, "I'll teach you how!" Nate Newton would take him out eating. Charles said he would try to eat with Nate, and when Nate ate chicken, he ate *all* the chicken. Then he'd eat all the bones! He said the marrow puts weight on you. Charles Mann said, "I couldn't do that." –*NFC Championship Game, Lions at Redskins (1/12/92)*

On the body fat of the Eagles defensive line: Reggie White thought he needed more strength in his arms and legs, so he went to Chicago and worked out with Al Vermeil, the strength coach for the Bulls. He said he's stronger in his arms and his legs now and has more explosion. When he came back, he had only ten-percent body fat. I mean, *ten-percent*! That sounds like something real little ol' skinny people have. [DT] Mike Golic says he *likes* fat, that fat's good. *You never heard of anybody pulling fat*. Billy Martin used to tell me that about baseball players. He said when he played, you never heard of baseball players pulling stuff. He said, "We didn't have any muscles to pull.

Now these guys got these big ol' arms and legs on them, and they're always pulling something." –*Eagles at Redskins (10/18/92)*

On a late-game sack by Cowboys DE Charles Haley: That's why they traded for Charles Haley. That's why they give him the big money. When you got a great player, great players have to make big plays when you need 'em…Once Haley gets by you, he really puts the burst on. Once he can smell the back of that number, and can see the name on the jersey, he is really gonna take that extra lunge. –*Cowboys at Broncos (12/6/92)*

On Cowboys DE Charles Haley causing a fumble: He hit Steve Young then kinda leg-whipped him around. I think he missed him with his hand, then he leg-whipped him and got him with his right knee and knocked the ball out of there with his right foot. I'll tell ya, Charles Haley knows how to raise havoc. He may not have great stats or a lot of sacks, but when you put him in on defense, he's a play-maker and a havoc-raiser. – *49ers at Cowboys (10/17/93)*

On Bears defensive end Richard Dent: [Lions T] Lomas Brown was saying yesterday that Dent is a tough guy to play against because he's big and strong and quick and he's got a pass rush. Then he said, "I've never figured this out: After the game he'll always say, 'Nice game. How's your wife? How's your kids?' If you cared about my wife and kids, why do you beat on me all day?" –*Bears at Lions (11/25/93)*

On Saints defensive lineman Robert Goff: [QB] Bobby Hebert said he went up to Goff when he first came to the team and said, "Hi, Robert." Goff said, "Don't call me Robert; my name's Pig." [Goff's] playing right in there in the pits and stuff… You try and run at him, but you're not gonna run over a guy named Pig. I'll guarantee you that. –*NFC Wildcard, Eagles at Saints (1/3/93)*

On 49ers defensive linemen looking at photographs: They take shots of the linemen from the endzone. Then the linemen will look at the different shots and plays and blocking schemes and all those things. When defensive linemen look at pictures, though, half of that is a bluff. They just get down there in the dirt and mud and roll around. They don't know what they're looking at. –*NFC Playoffs, Redskins at 49ers (1/9/93)*

On Cowboys DE Charles Haley: He's got one leg shorter than the other. That's why he walks sideways. He's 6-foot-3 on one side and 6-foot-4 on the other. –*NFC Championship Game, 49ers at Cowboys (1/23/94)*

On Cowboys DE Charles Haley being held by the Eagles: [T] Bernard Williams was beaten so badly and so quickly by Charles Haley that he had to do something; the last resort was to tackle him. That's what Haley brings to you. Haley causes havoc. He's like a bull in a china closet. He just runs in and stuff happens. –*Eagles at Cowboys (10/16/94)*

On Falcons DT Jumpy Geathers using the "forklift" move on G Aaron Taylor: Jumpy Geathers tried to give him that "forklift." Aaron Taylor says, "This guy is a tough guy to block. I've seen a lot of guys better than me that he's lifted up." You see how Geathers lifts him up? He just bent Aaron Taylor's back, then bent both of his knees. He has that move where he gets his right hand behind you, grabs your back, and pulls toward you. That will lift you up. Then he starts walking you back and collapsing you. On that play, he did all those things to Aaron Taylor. Any guard or center in this league – when you talk about who's the toughest guy to block, the best tackle – they always tell you "Jumpy Geathers." –*NFC Wildcard, Falcons at Packers (12/31/95)*

On Cowboys DE Charles Haley: He plays with leverage. He gets his helmet underneath his guy because the first thing you want to do is get your guy lifted up…He's either gonna use speed and go around a guy, or he's gonna make a quick move to the inside. You see what he did there? He had [Dolphins T] James Brown on the play before, where he jacked him up. He wants Brown to get ready for that. Then he's gonna hit him and take an inside move on him. Charles is like a boxer; everything he does is to set up the next thing he's gonna do. –*Cowboys at Dolphins (10/27/96)*

On 49ers DE Charles Haley's inside pass rush: Charles Haley will always come inside; that's why he's a great pass rusher. Average pass rushers are always *outside*. They take the beltway. Charles Haley will take the tough way, the inside. –*NFC Wildcard, Packers at 49ers (1/3/99)*

On Buccaneers DT Warren Sapp losing his helmet during a play: Some guys when they lose their hat, they just quit playing. Not Warren Sapp. When he gets a pass rush and it's third down, with or without a hat he's gonna keep coming. –*Giants at Buccaneers (11/24/03)*

On Colts DE Dwight Freeney being a dominant pass rusher indoors: Boy, is this Dwight Freeney *quick*. He's about as tough a defensive end that you could ever play against in a dome like this. You're playing inside, and he has this artificial turf and this crowd noise behind him. A guy who can move like Dwight Freeney is a nightmare for an offensive tackle…He has great knee-bend, and he can come around on a stunt and get right in front of a quarterback and make him throw that bad throw. –*Vikings at Colts (11/8/04)*

On Cowboys rookie DE Chris Canty: Chris Canty is going to be something special. I saw him in training camp. He's big and fast and quick and he has moves. Everyone was talking about Chris Canty as a young Leon Lett. Remember Leon Lett? That's what Chris Canty looks like – when Leon Lett was a young rookie or second-year guy. *–Redskins at Cowboys (9/19/05)*

Note: Over an eleven-year career, Canty was never voted All-Pro or named to the Pro Bowl.

Chapter 7: THE LINEBACKERS

Giants linebacker Lawrence Taylor destroys the Cowboy pass pocket.

On coaching against LB Bill Bergey: He was a rookie at Cincinnati, and we were having trouble blocking him. He was making all the tackles. Once, right in front of me, he made a tackle and I told [center] Jim Otto, "Doggonit, Jim, you have to get the middle linebacker blocked. You have to block Bergey!" Bergey says, "He can't do it! He's too old! He's too slow!" I knew right then I didn't have to say another word. Jim Otto did not let Bergey make another tackle the rest of the day. That was all he needed. –*Eagles at Cardinals (9/28/80)*

On Eagles LB Bill Bergey: He's the prototype of what a National Football League linebacker should be. He even looks intense when he's on the table getting taped. *That's* a real player. You chew tobacco, you have a beer, you spit on the floor. That's what linebacking is all about. –*Eagles at Seahawks (11/8/80)*

On why linebackers drop interceptions: They have tape on their hands and those pads on their arms, and they can never catch. They talk about it all week, how they're going to get an interception. Then they get all taped-up and padded-up and they drop them. –*Giants at 49ers (11/23/80)*

On Rams LB Jack Reynolds: All those linebackers are a little goofy. They all have that little glint in the eye. I'll guarantee you, Jack Reynolds has it. – *NFC Wildcard, Rams at Cowboys (12/28/80)*

On Giants LB Lawrence Taylor: He's the best rookie linebacker I've ever seen. –*Rams at Giants (12/6/81)*

On Giants LB Lawrence Taylor not performing as well in his second season: Sometimes they have that thing known as a sophomore jinx. You know what it is? The first year they don't know anything; they just react and play on instincts. Then they get a little knowledge and they start to think too much. They don't react like they did. I think Lawrence Taylor may be going through a little of that. –*Giants at Lions (11/25/82)*

On Raiders LB Matt Millen: Rich Milot, linebacker for the Redskins, played in college with Matt Millen. He was telling us when Millen played he wore one t-shirt all year – yellow. And it kept getting yellower and yellower as the year went on. It was the only shirt he wore. That's my kinda guy. One shirt. That's all ya need. –*Super Bowl XVIII, Redskins vs. Raiders (1/22/84)*

On eccentric Raiders LB Ted Hendricks: Ted Hendricks was a free spirit before there was such a thing. –*Rams at Raiders (12/18/82)*

On 49ers rookie LB Ron Ferrari: Ferrari played at Illinois for Mike White, who used to coach with Bill Walsh. He told Bill, "If you get Ferrari, he'll be the best special teams player you ever had." *Ferrari* – it sounds like a linebacker. *Hey Ferrari, get in there and hit 'em! –Raiders at 49ers (8/14/82)*

On Eagles LB John Bunting: He was looking for me yesterday. I guess last week against Dallas I said that he had a facemask penalty, and it wasn't him. We were in the locker room yesterday and he was trying to find me. That's why I left. I didn't want any confrontations in the locker room. There's nowhere to run. –*Giants at Eagles (1/2/83)*

On Giants LB Lawrence Taylor: When he blitzes *this* year, they don't put backs on him...They have him doubled with a tackle *and* a running back. A year ago, they used to block him with those running backs. That was a mismatch. That was your basic ace over a deuce. –*Giants at Eagles (1/2/83)*

On Giants LB Harry Carson: Bill Parcells was telling us yesterday that Harry Carson is the best linebacker he's ever seen against the reverse. He said Carson never gets fooled and always makes the play on a reverse. Parcells says that the guy that you teach, who reads all his keys, will usually be fooled by a reverse. The guy with great instincts *won't* be fooled, because he starts going one way, sees it, then just runs back the other way and tackles him. –*Giants at Cowboys (9/18/83)*

On Cowboys TE Doug Cosbie calling for pass interference: Cosbie is pointing at Lawrence Taylor, saying "Interference!" That wasn't interference. Taylor took a grab, but I don't think he caught him. You can *take* a grab, as long as you don't grab. –*Giants at Cowboys (9/18/83)*

On a diving tackle by Giants LB Lawrence Taylor: He can cover more ground with a dive than anyone I've ever seen. –*Cowboys at Giants (10/30/83)*

On a play in which Giants LB Lawrence Taylor disposed of two linemen then chased the QB out of bounds: We use the term *plays all-out...plays 100%.* They all don't do that, but this guy does. If you could get everyone to do that, the Giants wouldn't be 2-7-1. In fact, after they lost a game, Lawrence Taylor came to Bill Parcells and said, "I want to play offense, too." He wanted to play tight end, play both ways and play the whole game. That's not a bad idea. What they should do is stamp out a few more of him. A few of them play offense, a few play defense. Then they'd be okay. –*Redskins at Giants (11/13/83)*

On Giants LB Lawrence Taylor shattering a reverse: Joe Gibbs is saying right now, "Doggonit, if we're gonna run a reverse we probably shouldn't run it at Lawrence Taylor's side. He's too quick!" Taylor started to flow, but he's quick enough to come back, and he's waiting right there for Alvin Garrett. You can fool him a little, but the guy you *like* to fool is a guy that doesn't have a lot of quickness. Who starts in one direction and keeps going that way and can't get back. –*Redskins at Giants (11/13/83)*

On hearing that Giants LB Lawrence Taylor is taking up golf: The thing is, he can't play golf because they always tell linebackers to keep your head up and keep your eyes open. In golf, they tell you to keep your head *down*. Linebacker – keep your head up, see it, see it, *BOOM!* He's gonna go to the golf course and some guy is gonna say, "Keep your head down." –*Eagles at Giants (9/8/85)*

On an encounter with Broncos LB Tom Jackson: He used to hate me. He'd come over to the sideline and yell at me. I would yell at *him* from the sideline. Yesterday, he talked to me. I think the reason he talked to me was he had the flu and tried to give it to me. They've got the Taiwan flu going around this team...Suddenly, I suddenly thought he was a nice guy. *You get out, you're not coaching anymore, you're not competing. Everyone forgets. You* *shake hands.* Then I thought, *The last time I was here, he didn't talk to me; this time he came over and talked to me.* He said, "There's a lot of flu going around here. All the players have it. Don't talk to any of them. Don't let any of them breathe on you." Well, he *has* the flu! I was talking to him, and he was breathing on *me*! *–Redskins at Broncos (12/13/86)*

On Giants LB Lawrence Taylor: Wherever he goes, he kinda causes disturbances. *–NFC Championship Game, Redskins at Giants (1/11/87)*

On Giants LB Carl Banks: I think that Carl Banks went from being the other linebacker with Lawrence Taylor to being *Hey, you better look at this guy*, to being one of the best players in the league. The playoff game against the 49ers and the championship game against the Redskins are the two best games I've seen a linebacker play. *–Super Bowl XXI, Giants vs. Broncos (1/25/87)*

On Jets linebacker Troy Benson: Troy Benson is the brother of Brad Benson of the Giants. I'll bet you when his parents had those kids, they probably didn't think they'd be football players. If you were having a kid and you knew he was going to be a linebacker, why not name him something like *Whap*? Or *Ughh*? Give him a *linebacker* name. But Brad and Troy? I bet they didn't think they'd be pro football players. *–Eagles at Jets (12/20/87)*

On Saints undersized LB Sam Mills: Sam Mills is one of those guys who's built in a position to hit. He's only five-foot, nine-inches. You always say to a linebacker, "Get low. Stay low. Work from down to up." You say he's too short to play? Baloney! This guy can play. He's built in a hitting position. He walks the streets in a hitting position. *–Saints at 49ers (12/11/88)*

On sideline shot of 49ers LB Matt Millen celebrating a first down: Defensive guys love it when offensive guys control the ball by running it. Especially when it's a guy like [fullback] Tom Rathman, who looks like one of them. *–NFC Championship Game, Rams at 49ers (1/14/90)*

After a diving, dropped interception by linebacker Greg Manusky: I guarantee he'll get up and hit himself in the head. Yep, see that? He's a middle linebacker! Manusky! He wants "run." He doesn't want that passing stuff. He wants special teams. He wants contact. *Give me some guy to hit*! Then they throw him the ball, and he has no idea what the ball's all about. When he hit the ground, that was the best thing for him. *–Eagles at Redskins (10/21/90)*

On slow-motion replay of Chiefs LB Derrick Thomas rushing the QB: You wanna see a speed rush? Watch 58 here. He gets that shoulder down there and runs and runs and runs. Even when you go slow-motion, Derrick Thomas is fast. –*Redskins at Chiefs (11/15/92)*

After an explosive tackle by Bears linebacker Mike Singletary: Watch him at the end of this tackle. He always uncoils! He's gonna come across and tackle Daryl Johnston, but he just doesn't wrap his arms and take him down. Watch that explosion! You explode that shoulder in, *then* you wrap 'em up. Some guys just wrap 'em up; Singletary brings his whole load into you and *then* wraps you up. –*Bears at Cowboys (12/27/92)*

On Redskins linebacker Kurt Gouveia: The guy's instincts are so good. He really is an amazing player. He's not that big, he's not that strong, but he just has a great presence. And he has a good *name*. For a young kid, Gouveia is a good guy to be as a role model, because he's got all the vowels in his name – A, E, I, O, U. –*Redskins at Eagles (9/19/93)*

On Giants linebacker Lawrence Taylor: I don't know in my life if I've ever seen a more exciting defensive player than Lawrence Taylor. You could go on a practice field and you wouldn't have to say *Which one's Taylor?* If you just walked out there, you could feel him. –*Cowboys at Giants (1/2/94)*

On undersized Dolphins LB Nick Buoniconti: He was the toughest guy to block on a blitz. He was small, so he would get up there and hit that blitz-hole sideways. He wouldn't give you a lot to hit. Then, when he turned sideways and you'd try to block it, he'd kinda slither. If that's a football word. He would *slither* through the hole on a blitz. –*Bears at Dolphins (12/9/02)*

Chapter 8: DEFENSIVE BACKS

Redskins CB Darrell Green wrecks a pass play in Super Bowl XXII.

On Cowboys rookie free agent cornerback Everson Walls: [Coach] Tom Landry was saying, "I don't know how he does it. He doesn't have that much speed. His feet flop out. But he's always around the ball, and they don't complete 'em on him." –*Cowboys at Cardinals (10/4/81)*

More on Everson Walls: A year ago *everyone* was working on him... That guy is a player. Joe Gibbs says he has "athletic arrogance." I don't know what that means, but I like that kinda talk. –*Cowboys at Redskins (12/5/82)*

More on Everson Walls: Everson Walls is probably the most confident defensive back that I have ever seen. They say he can't run. He wasn't drafted. All he does is come in and wins a starting spot his first year, makes All-Pro and starts in the Pro Bowl. The guy is so confident. He gets out there like he can cover anyone. –*Giants at Cowboys (9/18/83)*

More on Everson Walls: This guy has the greatest hands of any defensive back that I've ever seen. –*Eagles at Cowboys (10/16/83)*

On Redskins cornerback Darrell Green: He can make up more space quicker than most guys. That's the secret. Guys can *run* fast, but you have to be able to make up space very quickly to be a corner. *–Giants at Redskins (12/17/83)*

On 49ers cornerback Ronnie Lott: Ronnie Lott says he loves to play man-to-man coverage. He said "Because I'm an athlete and I can use my athletic skills against another athlete." He doesn't like that zone defense. He says all you are is part of the scheme. "Man-to-man. Let me play against my man, my guy." *–NFC Championship Game, 49ers at Redskins (1/8/84)*

On Redskins' undersized cornerback Darrell Green: If Darrell Green isn't the Rookie of the Year defensively, he may be one of the best of the whole league as a corner. This guy is all over the place...Someone asked him, "What do you think when you have to come up and tackle?" He said, "I don't think anything. I just go up and tackle him." *–NFC Championship Game, 49ers at Redskins (1/8/84)*

On the '84 Redskins secondary: That's one thing about these Redskin corners, Darrell Green and Vernon Dean – they're good tacklers. A lot of corners are good cover guys and they don't get involved much in the run. But in the Redskin scheme of things, they use their corners as support guys. And they're *both* very good tacklers. *–Cardinals at Redskins (12/16/84)*

On 49ers cornerback Ronnie Lott facing Walter Payton: We were talking about Ronnie Lott and the intensity he has. He said to me that he thinks Walter Payton is the best back in football. But when Payton has the ball, he said, "I don't want to *show* respect. I just want to get to him, to make him respect *me*. Sometimes you can respect guys so much you just put 'em in awe and you don't do anything and they run right by you." He said that's not going to happen. *–NFC Championship Game, Bears at 49ers (1/6/85)*

On Cardinals cornerback Wayne Smith: Wayne Smith has quietly been having a pretty good year. If they don't throw the ball on you a lot, or catch a lot of passes on you, or you don't have any interference, they don't talk about you much. Sometimes a corner's best day is when his name isn't mentioned. *–Cardinals at Cowboys (11/28/85)*

On 49ers free safety Ronnie Lott: When the 49ers moved Ronnie Lott from corner to safety, they really picked up an extra linebacker in that middle. Because Lott never really *was* a corner. He'll even say that. He said, "I fooled 'em for a few years, but I'm a safety." I think he's about half a linebacker, also...That's the kinda guy you want, the guy that wants to get up and get in there. The guy you *worry* about is the guy that's back there but doesn't want to get into it. *–49ers at Redskins (12/8/85)*

On a leaping interception by Cowboys CB Everson Walls: Everson Walls can do two things better than most corners. One – he can time his jump, to get up there at the right time. And two – he has great hands to catch the ball. A lot of them can cover, a lot of them can knock 'em down, but Everson Walls can jump and catch 'em better than most. *–Cowboys at 49ers (12/22/85)*

On injuries: Of all the positions on a National Football League team, the one that you can *least* play while you have any injury is that cornerback spot. *–NFC Wildcard, 49ers at Giants (12/29/85)*

On a late sideline hit by Rams safety Johnny Johnson on Walter Payton: The fans are booing, Pat, but that's a tough one on Johnny Johnson. When you get on that sideline, you have to unload on Payton because you know he's going to unload on you. That's what Johnson's saying. *I just can't stand there and let him unload on me.* Now watch Walter as he goes out of bounds. He switches the ball and he's gonna unload with that right arm. So, Johnson has to get *his* load ready to go load-to-load. Some of the fans boo when you do that. But if a guy's loading up on you, you gotta load up on *him* or you go backwards. *–NFC Championship Game, Rams at Bears (1/12/86)*

On playing weight: One of the rules of a defensive back is, as you get older, you'd better get lighter. *–Giants at Raiders (9/21/86)*

On cornerbacks he feared most as a coach: When I was coaching there were three guys that I *never* messed with. Denver's Louis Wright was one, [Pittsburgh's] Mel Blount was the other, and Kansas City's Emmitt Thomas was the other. *–Cowboys at Broncos (10/5/86)*

On Bears safety Gary Fencik making an open-field tackle: They talk about him and his eleven years in the league and maybe he ought to retire. But this guy still makes big, big plays for this defense. That's a tough thing to do – an open-field tackle. I don't think there's anyone better at it than Fencik in open-field tackling. He leads the Bears. I mean, they have linebackers, they've got big guys, but Fencik from Yale leads them. *–Bears at Falcons (11/16/86)*

On Cowboys safety Bill Bates: Bill Bates is one of those guys who looks better in a uniform than he does in street clothes. Most guys look better in street clothes, but for some reason Bates looks better in his uniform. I don't know why. He ought to wear his uniform in the streets. In baseball there's some guys that look better in their uniform. In boxing some guys look better in their shorts than in their street clothes. Bates looks better in his uniform. *–Cowboys at 49ers (8/22/87)*

On Rams cornerbacks Jerry Gray and Leroy Irvin both making the Pro Bowl: When you get two cornerbacks in the Pro Bowl that play *all* zone defense, that's an amazing thing. Usually the cornerbacks that make the Pro Bowl are man-to-man cover guys. —*NFC Wildcard, Rams at Redskins (12/28/86)*

On Giants replacement player Steve Rehage: He made like every tackle last week. Bill Parcells said, "The only thing I'm worried about is the guy will be punch drunk. He made so many hits. He just runs around the field and launches his body into anything that's moving." Remember Doug Plank from the Bears? He was that way...those defensive backs that have total disregard for their bodies. —*Redskins at Giants (10/11/87)*

On a strong performance by 49ers safety Jeff Fuller: Jeff Fuller is the MVP of this first half, defensively. This guy's all over the field. He can run. He's up there making tackles. He has an interception already and almost had another one. He looks like a man possessed. He was close to making the All-Madden Team a couple of weeks ago, but I went to practice and caught him wearing pink shoes. *"BOOM!* You're out," I said. Now that he has the black shoes on again, he has a shot. We're still looking at him. —*NFC Championship Game, 49ers at Bears (1/8/89)*

On Cowboys veteran safety Bill Bates: Bill Bates is *always* the guy you're gonna replace [on the roster]. He's always the guy who can't run fast enough and all that stuff. Then you put him in the game and he starts hitting guys and you say, "Well, maybe Bates can still play." —*Cowboys at Chargers (8/13/89)*

On 49ers reserve defensive backs elevating their play: They say hitting is contagious. When you have an aggressive defense, *everyone* gets aggressive. You bring in a backup like [safety] Tom Holmoe; he's playing in there for Ronnie Lott. He comes in and *plays* like Ronnie Lott. You get a rookie like Johnny Jackson; he comes in and *plays* like Chet Brooks. Chet Brooks comes in and *plays* like Jeff Fuller after Fuller was injured. Those are the things that a championship team does. —*Bears at 49ers (12/24/89)*

After a hard sideline hit by 49ers safety Ronnie Lott: If he's gonna run all the way across the field and get you on the sideline, he's gonna bring the *full* load. He doesn't pursue and get all the way over there and just bring a quarter or half a load. When he gets there, he's gonna unload that whole thing he brought. —*NFC Championship Game, Rams at 49ers (1/14/90)*

On Eagles cornerback Eric Allen's drooping socks: Eric Allen's been running so much today, I think he's run out of his *socks*. He's been chasing guys. The Redskins have a guy on him every time. When your legs start to get tired – I'm not kidding ya, I've had defensive backs tell me – those socks start to feel heavy. They want to take their socks off. They want to let their legs breathe. I know, you say your legs can't breathe. But those guys *believe* that. I swear they do. *–Eagles at Redskins (10/21/90)*

On Packers safety Chuck Cecil: There's a guy that'll hit ya. You talk about one of the tough guys in the NFL.... In fact, he hits so hard a lot of times he darn near self-destructs. He hurts himself. He gets a lot of injuries because he hits so hard. He just zeros in and throws his body at anything wearing the other color jersey. *–Packers at Eagles (12/16/90)*

On 49ers safety Ronnie Lott hammering a receiver over the middle: He's the guy that lifts this whole team. Ronnie Lott is the guy that brings it up with hits like this, in games like this. You're not gonna run a post in there and not get *this* at the end of it when number 42 is sitting there. Now if you do something to get him outta there, you have a chance. But I'll guarantee you, when you throw it in [the middle] and you don't run him outta there, he's gonna do *that*, and he's gonna lift the whole 49er defense. *–NFC Championship Game, Giants at 49ers (1/20/91)*

On 49ers cornerback Mark Lee: The Raiders really haven't worked on him. He kinda expected it today. He's a 12-year veteran. He learned that, in the National Football League, they work on you on your way *in*, and they work on you on your way *out*. He said, "When you're in the middle, they kinda leave you alone." They [typically] work on rookies and old guys. *–49ers at Raiders (9/29/91)*

On Redskins CB Darrell Green: He's not only fast – the fastest man in the NFL – but he's so quick. We were talking to [Cowboys QB] Troy Aikman and he said, "You look over at the guy he's covering and you never see much *air* between the jerseys." That's tough to throw to. That doesn't give you a lot of confidence when you see the white jersey 28 just blending in with the blue jersey of *your* guy. *–Cowboys at Redskins (11/24/91)*

On a bad day for Redskins CB Darrell Green: I don't know that I've ever seen a team throw and complete as many passes on Darrell Green as the Cowboys have today. Even though that last one, that 20- yarder, didn't [count] because of the penalty, Green has given them confidence. And when you've given them confidence, it's like sending out an invitation. They're gonna keep doing it until you stop one of those things. Darrell Green has to knock one down or pick one off or they're gonna keep working on him. *– Cowboys at Redskins (11/24/91)*

On a futile tackle attempt by Giants CB Mark Collins: Look at how big [RB] Keith Byars is! He's so big and strong! He weighs over 240 pounds. Collins comes up to tackle him and it's like he runs into a fire hydrant. He didn't move him at all. He just knocked Byars' towel out. The whole body stays there, and the only thing that flies out is a little towel. That's embarrassing. Here you are, Mark Collins, you come up and *BOOM*! You're gonna give it your best shot, and all that flies out is a towel. Nothing happens to Byars. – *Eagles at Giants (12/8/91)*

On Redskins CB Darrell Green: The only way you can beat Darrell Green is on a double-move. A single move can't beat Darrell Green. –*Lions at Redskins (9/20/92)*

On Eagles strong safety Andre Waters: Joe Gibbs was talking about Andre Waters last night. He said, "The amazing thing about Waters is he could be ten or twelve yards deep and you would think he couldn't get there, and he'd *still* make the tackle at the line of scrimmage." –*Redskins at Eagles (12/20/92)*

On Eagles safety Wes Hopkins: One thing they do on this level, a little better than they do in college, is tackle. A guy like Wes Hopkins is one of the best tackling safeties in football. He's one of the best tackling safeties that ever *played*. I remember when they used to have Hopkins and Andre Waters back there. They were darn near like having two extra linebackers in there. – *Redskins at Eagles (9/19/93)*

On a replay of a smashing hit by Redskins 5-8 CB Darrell Green: He looks like a new man! When he first came in the league, they thought he was too small. He's been in the league eleven years, and he's playing today like he just got here. He made, in the first half, two of the greatest interceptions that I've ever seen. And here – I don't remember Darrell Green *ever* hitting like this. He's hitting like some fierce linebacker. They might have to rule him right out of this league. This guy's dangerous out there! –*Redskins at Eagles (9/19/93)*

On 49ers CB Deion Sanders' spindly legs: We saw Deion Sanders yesterday in practice. He was wearing dress socks and he had his pants pulled up above his knees. Those legs did *not* look like the legs of a great athlete.... Everyone would look at him. They were pointing to his legs and socks. I think he wears four or five pairs of socks during the game [to beef up his legs]. – *49ers at Chargers (12/11/94)*

On Cowboys cornerback Deion Sanders: One of the things the Steelers said was, "We're not gonna worry about Deion Sanders. We're gonna go after him. We're gonna treat him like any other corner." I don't know that you can *treat* him like any other corner, because he covers like no other corner covers. But if you stay away from him completely, then you play right into their hands and give the Cowboys the strength of an extra man. *–Cowboys at Steelers (8/31/97)*

On the qualities of an NFL cornerback: To be a corner in this league, you have to have a pretty good dose of cockiness and a bad memory. Anything bad that happens to you, you have to forget about it. And you have to believe that no one can beat you. That's why I think some of those corners are so demonstrative, 'cause they're kinda *talking* themselves into it. *–Eagles at Cowboys (9/3/00)*

On Steelers strong safety Troy Polamalu: You listen to Troy Polamalu and he sounds like a gentle guy. *Off* the field he is. He gets *on* the field and he's a totally different guy. This guy is all over the place. He'll launch himself at everything. [Steelers defensive coordinator] Dick LeBeau says the thing to look for in a great safety is a guy who can sack the quarterback *and* intercept the ball deep. That's Troy Polamalu. *–Super Bowl XL, Steelers vs. Seahawks (2/5/06)*

Chapter 9: SPECIAL TEAMS

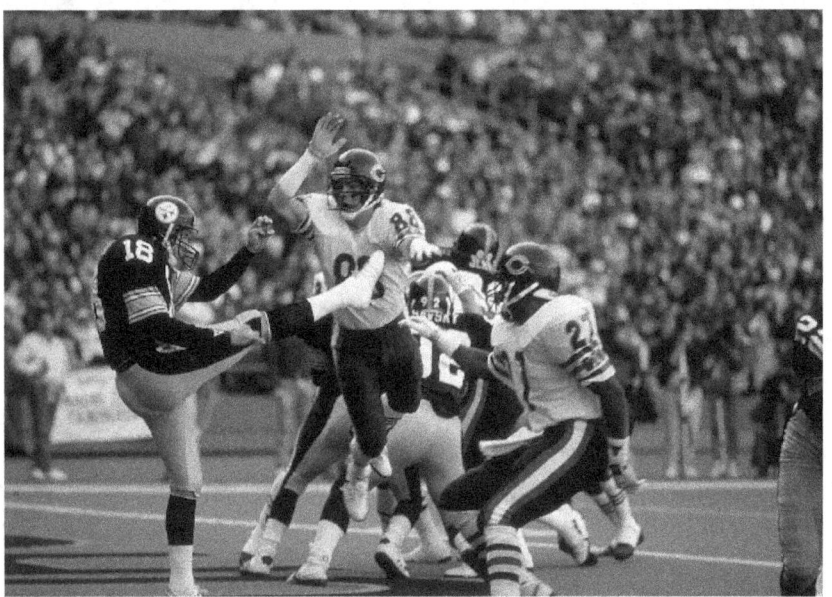

The Bears throw a heavy charge at Steelers punter Harry Newsome.

If there's any one thing, early in the season, that wins or loses football games it's the play of special teams. –*Falcons at Patriots (9/14/80)*

On clipping penalties during the kickoff: As a coach, that used to drive you crazy. I finally put in a rule. I told my men, "Men, if you can read their name, don't block them." Then I changed that. I said, "If you can *see* their name, don't block them." We had some kickers with funny names. –*Falcons at Patriots (9/14/80)*

On why kickers are so uptight: It happens because they have so long between plays. They try a field goal or an extra point or a punt, then they have to go over to the sideline for ten minutes, sometimes fifteen minutes, sometimes three quarters, and they have all this time to think. I really think *all* kickers think too much. –*Eagles at Cardinals (9/28/80)*

On Eagles placekicker Tony Franklin: Any guy that kicks sideways and barefooted has to be a pretty good guy. I was telling him that my son was a kicker. He said, "Does he kick barefooted?" I said "No, he's a pretty normal kid." –*Eagles at Redskins (11/16/80)*

On why kickers shouldn't look at the goal posts before FG tries: That's what we used to teach. The hash marks run right down [the middle of the field], and the goal posts are an *extension* of the hash marks. If you look up at the goal posts, they look so narrow when you're kicking a field goal. But if you look at the hash marks and try to kick in that width *between* the hash marks, it's a lot easier. And, it keeps your head down. –*Giants at 49ers (11/23/80)*

On punters warming up: I used to hate to see my punter warming up on first down. I'd say, "Doggonit, have confidence! Sit down!" –*Cardinals at Giants (11/30/80)*

On kickers: No one understands kickers. No one. I'm *interested* in kickers and I like them, but I don't understand them. No one does. They don't even understand themselves. –*Falcons at Eagles (12/7/80)*

On why teams have kickoff problems late in the season: It's not hard for me to understand, because kickers get tired also. At the end of the season kickers' legs get tired, and it shows on kickoffs. That takes everything they have. The most kickoffs a kicker can practice in a day is about five; they don't even like *that* because it takes everything they have in their leg. –*Falcons at Eagles (12/7/80)*

On Raiders punter Ray Guy: He's probably the most flexible person I have ever seen. That's why, when he has physical problems, it's always in his back, the lower back...from getting into some of those positions he keeps getting into. –*Buccaneers at Raiders (10/18/81)*

On Packers kicker Jan Stenerud: I coached Stenerud many times in the Pro Bowl. All the other kickers had to have the special holder, the snap, *Get the ball down. Do this. Do that.* Jan would say, "Just put the ball down and I'll kick it." I always appreciated that. –*Giants at Packers (11/8/81)*

On Eagles barefoot kicker Tony Franklin: Only *kickers* would do anything barefoot. You'd never see a barefoot quarterback or guard or nose tackle. –*Giants at Eagles (11/22/81)*

On how Raiders kicker George Blanda checked wind direction on artificial turf: He always took a little piece of paper with him. –*Giants at Eagles (11/22/81)*

On punting and the wind: The idea, when you kick *with* the wind, is to get it up in the air; when you kick *against* the wind, you try and kick a line drive. –*Rams at Giants (12/6/81)*

On why punters aren't very popular: Because every time they come in, something bad just happened. If the offense is *successful* on third down, then they don't come in. If it's third down and they *don't* make the first, the punter comes in. That's why no one likes them. –*Falcons at Giants (9/12/82)*

On Falcons punter Dave Smigelsky: Smigelsky. That'd be a good name for a linebacker. *At middle linebacker – Smigelsky! Smigelsky at the bottom of the pile!* Not a punter. Bad name for a punter. Good name for a middle linebacker. –*Falcons at Giants (9/12/82)*

On Eagles kicker Tony Franklin making the tackle on a kickoff: MADDEN: That may be the first time in his life Tony Franklin has made a tackle. He looked like a *linebacker*, though. He looked good. Bent his knees, head down. Got a little backward summersault, but he bent those knees. See that?

SUMMERALL: After *that* lick, Tony will be sore for the rest of the offseason.

MADDEN: He'll have lots to talk about, though. He'll say, "Boy, it's tough in the trenches." –*Giants at Eagles (1/2/83)*

On Vikings punter Greg Coleman: Greg Coleman said, to him, the perfect kick is all fours – 44 yards, 4.4 hang time. –*Cowboys at Vikings (10/2/83)*

On Dallas QB/punter Danny White: Danny White says he likes to punt. Being the quarterback, he says if something bad happens, he can take it out on the ball on the punt. Usually when he has to punt, something bad *did* happen or he wouldn't be punting. He said he'd take it out on the ball. WHACK! *Take that, you ball!* –*Cowboys at Giants (10/30/83)*

On Falcons kicker Mick Luckhurst: I was watching television in the offseason one Saturday night. I'm watching this PKA boxing. I look up and there is *Luckhurst* in the ring! He's *fighting* a guy! Kickboxing! Any guy who's goofy enough to kick is probably goofy enough to PKA. –*Falcons at Rams (10/7/84)*

On Giants special teamer Joe McLaughlin: MADDEN: *There's* a typical special teams player. Those kinda guys that play linebacker, got a little moustache, weird look in their eyes. The first time they played Tampa Bay, [NT] Jim Burt told McLaughlin that Sean Farrell, the guard of the Buccaneers, doesn't like cats. So, McLaughlin made a noise all day like he was a cat – *Hissssss! Hissssss!*

SUMMERALL: Farrell asked Burt after the game, "Is that guy crazy?"

MADDEN: Burt said, "No, he just thinks he's a cat." Burt made up that story, that Sean Farrell doesn't like cats, so McLaughlin acted like a cat. –*Cardinals at Giants (11/18/84)*

On Redskins FG kicker Mark Moseley tying his shoe late in the game: How can a kicker do that? He doesn't do *anything* else. All he does is kick. Mosely doesn't kick off. How come you have to tie your shoe when you get to *this* point in the game? What else have you been doing all day? – *Cardinals at Redskins (12/16/84)*

On a scuffle between 49ers punter Max Runager and Giants DB Elvis Patterson: There's one thing you don't see often – a punter trying to get into a fight. I think he got hit late. Here he comes, number 4. [Punters] aren't the most physical guys. Here comes Elvis Patterson. He hits him. Runager says, "What'd you do that for?" Then he gave him a little rap. That's a punter's little rap, that push there. Those guys are getting *violent* out there. We've gotta stop the violence in punters. –*NFC Playoffs, Giants at 49ers (12/29/84)*

On Giants punter Sean Landeta's single-bar facemask: He has to be a spitter. You see that facemask, the single bar? It was all dirty on the inside. The only way you can get dirty on the inside of a facemask is spitting stuff out. If you're a *real* player, then it gets dirty from the outside-in. If you're a kicker who spits, it's dirty on the inside. –*Eagles at Giants (9/8/85)*

On the Giants' poor kickoff coverage: Bill Parcells was so upset last week with his kickoff coverage that he told them in a meeting, "If you guys don't do better this week, *three* of you are going to be cut. Three of you guys are going. I already know who I'm bringing in, and I'll tell you who they are." He told them two of the guys and said, "You don't know the third guy, but I'm bringing them in." So now on kickoff coverage, there's a tryout every time they run down the field. –*Giants at Saints (10/27/85)*

On Cowboys Bill Bates' aggressiveness on punt returns: Bates will *find* a tackler. *Where are those tacklers? Let me at 'em!* –*Bears at Cowboys (11/17/85)*

On the un-kickerlike qualities of Bears Kevin Butler: We're watching Kevin Butler walk off the field and he's chewing tobacco. You talk about treacherous things. Imagine kicking the ball and trying to run down there if somebody blocks you.... Butler, who's a rookie, hangs out with the offensive line. He's got the chewing tobacco, sleeves rolled up, pads on his arms. But he's still a kicker. –*Falcons at Bears (11/24/85)*

On Bears punter Maury Buford: Did you see Buford sneeze? I think that's the first time I've ever seen a guy sneeze before he punted. –*Bears at Jets (12/14/85)*

On using starters on special teams: You always want your best athletes on special teams. That's your first thought. Your second thought is, "I hope they don't get hurt." –*NFC Wildcard, 49ers at Giants (12/29/85)*

On Saints kicker Morten Anderson celebrating after a long field goal: It seems like kickers like those long ones, don't they? Because they don't have the pressure. They're really not expected to make it. *Let's go from 53; if you miss it, so what?* They can get that adrenaline pumping and – BOOM! – get everything into it. –*Saints at Jets (10/26/86)*

On Giants punter Sean Landeta's tight-fitting helmet: Doesn't Landeta's helmet always look like it's squeezing his head? There's not a scratch on that helmet. That helmet hasn't had contact. But if it ever did, it would just squeeze and squeeze and your eyes may pop out. You look at [LB] Gary Reasons – good helmet, good facemask on there. Looks like it's not too tight. Zeke Mowatt, big facemask. Landeta's looks like it's squeezing. Maybe he has less helmet and more forehead. There's more forehead and stuff sticking out. –*Giants at Eagles (11/9/86)*

On a bouncing kickoff that carried into the endzone: That kick went right through everyone. It didn't hit anything, so the clock didn't start. I used to play a pinball machine that way. I always wondered why sometimes it would go all the way down and hit nothing and go right into the hole. I didn't even get the flipper to work. I was so shocked that it didn't hit anything that my fingers didn't flip. That kickoff went just like the ball going through the pinball machine and not hitting anything. –*Packers at Lions (11/27/86)*

On Giants kicker Raul Allegre: Raul Allegre said the biggest problem he had when he came to the Giants was finding a pair of shoulder pads small enough to fit him. He said he went to Toys-R-Us to get them. –*Giants at Steelers (9/5/87)*

On firing up his Raiders special teams: I used to say things like, "Special teams breeds fanaticism." Then I'd say, "Go out there and be fanatic!" Then I had to change it to "*controlled* fanaticism" because I had penalties all the time. Clips and late hits and upside-downs and out-of-bounds. I changed it and said, "Special teams breeds *controlled* fanaticism." I didn't have anyone on the team that knew what fanaticism meant. –*Cowboys at Giants (9/20/87)*

On Cowboys kicker Roger Ruzek "banking" in a field goal: I've always thought this kicking was easy. You start here on the right hash-mark and you just kick it here over to this post. Anyone can kick it straight through, but it takes real talent to hit it here and bank it in. The old bank shot...*Hit it right here, bank it here, whap it into here, and you get three points for it.* That's the way Willie Moscone told me you do it. –*Vikings at Cowboys (11/26/87)*

On punt blocks: [Redskins punter] Steve Cox was saying an interesting thing. He said, "As a punter, you never *see* a punt block, but you hear that second thump. When you kick it, you hear one *Thump*. When you hear *Thump, THUMP*, you know it's a bad one." –*Cowboys at Redskins (12/13/87)*

On making the final roster cut: In the last preseason game, the way you can tell who's gonna make the team is by who plays on special teams. –*Eagles at Dolphins (9/2/89)*

On Redskins special teamer Greg Manusky: Greg Manusky sounds like a special teams player, a coverage guy. He looks like one. He runs like one. He acts like one. He has a haircut like one. He plays like one. He tackles like one. After all that, he'll get up and have a smile on his face. That's how you know he's a "Manusky!" –*Redskins at Saints (10/1/89)*

On Giants LB Carl Banks scoring on a fake field goal: They needed a big play here. When you're playing the Eagles, in your division on the road, you gotta make things happen. Drop a pass on third down, then you come right back with a gutsy, gutsy, gutsy call. On one play a wide receiver, Odessa Turner, drops it on third down. So you throw it to your linebacker on fourth down. He's got gloves and pads and probably some sweat and dirt, and he [still] catches the thing. Linebackers can make tackles, they can make sacks, but when they catch a pass and score a touchdown, that's the highlight of their football life. –*Giants at Eagles (10/8/89)*

On the kicking Zendejas Brothers – Max, Luis and Tony: Anyone who has had a lot of kickers on their team, somewhere along the line, has had a Zendejas. I think there's like thirteen of them. I think half the teams in the NFL have a Zendejas. Luis Zendejas has signed with the Cowboys four different times. –*Eagles at Cowboys (11/23/89)*

On a replay of Giants special teams ace Reyna Thompson: It's why he's the best cover guy in the league. The Rams are gonna put two men on him. They bang him, they block him, they hold him, they grab him.... He's still gonna make the tackle – *BOOM!* He's not only the best in the game today, but he's the best cover guy I've *ever* seen. –*Giants at Rams (11/11/90)*

On Saints kicker Morten Anderson botching a kickoff: He goes right into a pout, an immediate pout. He picked up and threw the tee like it was the tee's fault. Kickers are like golfers; they blame everything except themselves. *I don't know what's wrong with my nine-iron today*. Nothing's wrong with your nine-iron. It's you! –*NFC Wildcard, Saints at Bears (1/6/91)*

On kicker Matt Bahr's tackling technique: The first thing you do is come up and square-up, then you unload your load. *BOOM*! You let him have it. Exactly what Matt Bahr did. That's a pretty good tackle. But you never, ever put your head down. A kicker is like a golfer – you're always taught to keep your head down. But when you're *tackling*, you *never* put your head down. – *NFC Playoffs, Bears at Giants (1/13/91)*

On kicking the ball through the endzone on kickoffs: Two groups love that – the special teams that have to cover the kick, and the defense. Because every good defense believes that no team can go eighty yards on them. –*Bears at Saints (10/27/91)*

On a whirling, futile punt return by Bears Tom Waddle: Waddle's not fast enough to make that change of direction. That's the old thing Hugh McIlhenny used to do – reverse his field. Waddle's too slow for that kind of run. He tried to do a reverse-the-field and he just did a pirouette or something…This is one thing you never, ever do if you don't have speed. You don't go in circles. Never has one guy run so far for so long and so slow and taken so many divots on a play in the history of the National Football League. –*Lions at Bears (11/3/91)*

On shot of punter Kelly Goodburn groping the football: You notice how kickers always squeeze the ball? The NFL always uses brand new footballs, so the kickers and punters are always trying to loosen them up and soften them so they don't kick what they call a "stiff ball." The only guys that ever do that are the kickers. They're responsible. Quarterbacks always want the kickers to *rub* it good for them. None of it helps. They're all goofy. –*Eagles at Redskins (10/18/92)*

On punting in Denver's Mile High Stadium: Ray Guy, who was one of the greatest punters who ever punted a ball, would always look forward to coming to Denver because of the altitude thing. *Boy, you could really boom one*. And he would over-swing or over-power and he never did have a big day here. Yet they're always reminding you that this is Mile High Stadium, where the air is thin and the ball will really carry. –*Cowboys at Broncos (12/6/92)*

On Cowboys rookie kicker Lin Elliott: I think Jimmy Johnson has found a kicker that he likes. Any time, early in the season, that you make a decision to go with a rookie kicker, and you have a team that can make the playoffs…be in the playoffs…maybe be in the championship game…maybe be in the Super Bowl, that's a real tough decision. –*Cowboys at Broncos (12/6/92)*

On the specter of a missed extra point: Any time you miss an extra point, or the extra point is blocked, it seems like that thing sits up there on the scoreboard all day on ya. It's like eating a dumpling or something. It just sits in your stomach. –*Cowboys at Broncos (12/6/92)*

On kickers warming up while the offense is near the endzone: MADDEN: I used to hate it when the kicker would warm up when you had a first down at the ten-yard line.

SUMMERALL: That's one thing I *never* did.

MADDEN: No, you never let 'em do that. Don't be thinking field goal. If he says, "I'm warming up for the extra point," that's all right.

SUMMERALL: He shouldn't *have* to warm up for the extra point.

MADDEN: That's the *other* point! That's why he shouldn't be warming up! –*NFC Championship, Cowboys at 49ers (1/17/93)*

On tackling on special-teams: The good ones have a feel of weaving their way through and getting down there without getting blocked. The bad ones don't *want* to get down there. They always find a way to get blocked. –*Redskins at Eagles (9/19/93)*

On Redskins punter Reggie Roby outkicking his coverage: His first kick as a Redskin, he punted the ball and – *BOOM!* – they ran it all the way back for a touchdown. They said the hang time was too long. I remember years ago when I had Ray Guy. I used to tell Guy, "You kick it as high, as hard, as far as you can. If they can't cover it, I'll get new guys that *can* cover it." I also used to tell my quarterback, "You *can't* throw it too hard. Throw it as hard as you can up the field. If they can't catch it, I'll get new guys." –*Redskins at Eagles (9/19/93)*

On Cowboys special teams fanatic Bill Bates: Bates may not be the fastest guy on the team, but if he's not the fastest guy on the team, how does he get to be the first guy down there all the time? Special teams is ninety percent wanting-to. Look at him! He comes like he's shot out of a cannon. And when he's shot out of a cannon, he's going for something. He looks like a whirling dervish. –*Eagles at Cowboys (10/16/94)*

On finding toughness: If you want to find out where the toughest guys are that don't play every down, look on kick coverage and punt coverage. – *Cowboys at Giants (12/24/94)*

On diminutive Buccaneers kicker Martín Gramática: This doesn't look like a real kicker. You look at Martin Gramática in that uniform and wonder if that's really an NFL uniform. It looks like it could be a Halloween costume. I don't think that's an NFL player *or* an NFL uniform. If you put this picture of Gramática up and said, "Is this an NFL player or a trick-or-treat costume for Halloween?" I'd pick trick-or-treating. –*Buccaneers at Vikings (9/30/01)*

On what it's like to kick a football in sub-zero weather: Did you ever kick a bag of bolts? –*Vikings at Packers (11/21/05)*

On Broncos stubby fullback Cecil Sapp returning a kickoff: You know you don't have speed when you're running forward, looking backward, putting both hands on the ball, and knowing you're about to get caught. – *Chargers at Broncos (11/19/06)*

Chapter 10: STADIUMS & OFFICIALS

Cleveland Browns LB Eddie Johnson shows the ref a piece of his mind.

On referees signaling "inches short" of a first down: I was always upset when the referees made that sign. I thought they were telling everyone in the stadium and everyone watching on television, "That's all they have to go." Especially when it was fourth down and you had to send your punting team in. I used to just tell them, "You don't have to say how much we have to go! Either it's a first down or it's not! That's all you have to do!" –*Madden's first CBS telecast, Saints at 49ers (9/23/79)*

On artificial turf: I never did like it, but it does dry a lot easier than natural grass. –*Falcons at Patriots (9/14/80)*

On being booed in Kansas City: Years ago, I coached a Pro Bowl here at Arrowhead. We were the home team. And the biggest boo of the night was for me. I said, "Wait, I'm the *home* team! I'm the coach here!" –*Lions at Chiefs (10/26/80)*

On why officials no longer wear triple-digits on their jerseys: At that time, when they added new officials, they didn't have enough numbers, so they started giving them hundred-numbers. I told an official once that he couldn't know what he was talking about because he had three digits on his back. He said he was so self-conscious about that, that they went to the league and said they ought to change the numbering system. –*Cardinals at Giants (11/30/80)*

On a poor home performance by the Giants: A lot of the fans have left, and as some were leaving a guy yelled up to me, "Too bad, John, you have to stay and watch it!" –*Eagles at Giants (9/6/81)*

On the balance of penalties in a game: The biggest thing in penalties is, you can accept as many as the other team has. It's the *difference* between the two. If you have ten and they have ten, that's no problem. If you have ten and they have none, that's a big problem. –*Giants at Redskins (9/13/81)*

On artificial turf: That's what's wrong with artificial turf: The rain doesn't make mud. –*Eagles at Cowboys (12/13/81)*

On the sterility of artificial turf: You get some rain on those facemasks. But what you need in there is a little mud and a little dirt and a little grass hanging down there between those bars. That's the trouble with this artificial turf. Everyone stays too clean. –*Eagles at Cowboys (12/13/81)*

On shirtless fans in freezing conditions: There's a lot of guys in these stadiums whose elevators don't go all the way to the top. –*NFC Wildcard, Giants at Eagles (12/27/81)*

On coaching at Denver's Mile High Stadium: One of the things that you can't adjust to is the altitude here. We did a lot of studies. When you play in Denver, do you come in early and try to get adjusted to it? They say there's no way that you can. So, we would come in as late as we can, then get out as early as we can, and spend as little time as we can. And bring a lot of oxygen tanks. –*49ers at Broncos (9/19/82)*

On the officials debating a spot of the ball: The first thing to go are the eyes. –*Redskins at Giants (11/21/82)*

After a failed Eagles third-down play: There are good boo-ers here in Philadelphia. –*Giants at Eagles (1/2/83)*

On muddy RFK Stadium: I like to see a little rain out there. Look at [RB] Ottis Anderson walking back. It's the first quarter. He's got mud on his pants and stuff. That's football to me. Some good dirt, some mud…that's the way it should be. –*Cardinals at Redskins (12/16/84)*

On a deep sideline throw by 49ers QB Joe Montana: The 49ers don't practice throwing deep because they *can't*. They only have one practice field.

Half of it is artificial turf; the other half is mud. So, they never practice in the mud. They just practice in the artificial turf. So, if they're on the 20, they can only throw the ball thirty yards anyway [or they're into the mud]. *–NFC Championship Game, Bears at 49ers (1/6/85)*

On phoniness: The three phoniest things in football are the wave, artificial turf and domed stadiums. In that order. *–Eagles at Giants (9/8/85)*

Excusing the 777 no-shows at Green Bay's Lambeau Field: They've got a lot of farmers around here, and sometimes the hogs or cattle [need attention]. The cows need milking and stuff. You never know what's gonna come up with them on a Saturday night or Sunday morning. *–Giants at Packers (9/15/85)*

On a dopey fan wearing a toy Jets helmet: That helmet has *never* been in a football game, I'll guarantee ya. That thing is what you call a prop. It could've been a lamp or something. It was probably in the den and the guy took it off and put it on to come to the game. *–Bears at Jets (12/14/85)*

On getting hurt in cold weather: One thing about being cold is when you get stung a little, it stings more than "stung a little." At ten degrees "stung a little" stungs a lot. *–NFC Playoffs, Giants at Bears (1/5/86)*

On the NFL's new Instant Replay procedure: Bill Parcells was saying that one of the guards at Giants Stadium told him, "This is really getting to be an event, isn't it, this instant replay? It's kinda like paying alimony, and then having to sit around to see if the rabbit dies." *–Giants at Seahawks (10/19/86)*

On a "Trying to Consume Time" penalty called on Giants safety Kenny Hill: They're gonna say he didn't let [RB] Keith Griffin up. The Redskins were trying to go without a huddle and get back to the line of scrimmage, and Kenny Hill wasn't gonna let him up. You see, it's not "Unnecessary Roughness." It's just "Trying to Consume Time." He's not doing anything. There's no combilations in there. There's no foreign objects. No one's coming off the top ring. He's not giving him the business down there. All he's doing is "consuming time." That was a good play; he just consumed some stuff.... If you're like Kenny Hill and you're from Yale, you get penalties like that. Consumption penalties. *–Giants at Redskins (12/7/86)*

NOTE: "Combilations" is a reference to a gibberish word once used by Dallas coach Tom Landry.

On L.A. Rams fans: These fans don't get real excited out here. I know your team's down. Your team just lost Eric Dickerson [in a trade], I know that. They just kinda come and sit here and watch it, win or lose. No one's really upset. They're just having a nice day. Even if they do [have something to get excited about], they don't get real excited here. It's close to Disneyland...the beach. *—49ers at Rams (11/1/87)*

On referee Johnny Grier asking the wild Giants Stadium crowd to "refrain from the noise": I'll tell ya, that's not gonna do it. Some of these people don't know what "refrain" means. If you know what refrain means, you shouldn't be a football fan. *—Rams at Giants (9/25/88)*

On the impact of wind: In a football game, the worst thing is the wind. Wind is always worse than cold or snow or rain or anything. *—NFC Championship Game, 49ers at Bears (1/8/89)*

On kickers changing their official "range" on long FGs: Those kickers have a way of telling you during the game *I can do it*. On Friday and Saturday they say, "I don't know...I got a little twinge...I got *this*...." Then they're in the game and they've got adrenaline and they add another 15 yards. *—Eagles at Rams (9/23/90)*

On a day of blown field goals at RFK Stadium: I don't think I remember anything like this. The Eagles have missed two, the Redskins four. That's *six* field goals! We checked the goals posts in between and they're the right width, so it's not the goal posts. The field looks in as good a condition as I've ever seen it. What else is there for excuses? The holders? The only thing I can think of is...*when's Halloween?* I think we're getting close. I don't know when it is, but I've seen a lot of pumpkins and brooms and stuff out. I think that's the thing in the air that's doing it. *—Eagles at Redskins (10/21/90)*

On the definition of perfect football weather: You know why you can never say it's a perfect day for football? It depends on who you are. Big guys like cold days...the big, old, strong, heavy guys. The little, light guys like the hot days. There's no perfect day for everyone.... I was telling Bears kicker Kevin Butler this weather feels great. He said, "Oh, no! It's windy! Those golfers [in the Greater Milwaukee Open] are having a heckuva time with this wind. It won't be good to kick in!" So, it all depends on who you are and what you think is good weather. *—Vikings at Bears (9/1/91)*

On Saints kicker Morten Anderson's use of "Cognitive Intervention": MADDEN: We were talking to Morten Anderson yesterday, and he said kicking is ninety-percent mental. He said, "When you're on the sideline, you always want to keep busy because you don't want negative thoughts to come into your head. You're always doing positive images." He said that's what he does when he's there on the sideline – *cognitive* *intervention*. Now *that* has to come from a kicker. There's no nose tackles worried about cognitive intervention.

SUMMERALL: *That* comes from a guy who has a lot of free time.

MADDEN: He's going back to the sideline for the cognitive intervention. I'll guarantee you these guys down here in the pits don't know about cognitive intervention.

SUMMERALL: I don't remember that *I* had it or used it when *I* was playing.

MADDEN: In the days that you were playing, kickers used to get dirty. They used to have mud and dirt and stuff hanging on them. Now they're clean. I think kicker cleanliness and cognitive intervention go together. *–49ers at Saints (11/10/91)*

On choosing the proper footwear: One of the problems a visiting team has is not knowing the field. When I coached, I used to always like to go in a day early and practice on the field, for just one reason – to get used to your shoes. Just to get the right shoes, to get used to the turf, to decide what shoes you're gonna wear. Because that's such a big part of being able to play this game. *–Eagles at 49ers (11/29/92)*

On the white cap of the referee: MADDEN: Is there anything plainer in the world than a referee's cap? How would you buy one of those? Would you go in there and say, "Just give me a plain white cap?" I don't think anyone has ever bought one of those caps except the referee.

SUMMERALL: They used to wear black hats. I think it made them seem too evil.

MADDEN: At least the black caps have white stripes. White is about as plain as you can get. I think [Cowboys coach] Jimmy Johnson would like to get his *hands* on that white cap. *–49ers at Cowboys (10/17/93)*

On the cramped Oakland-Alameda County Stadium training room: I thought it was a big training room [when I coached here]. I looked at it again yesterday and said, "Jeez, you can only fit about three or four guys in there." My philosophy was, if you had a little training room and no one could get in there, then no one would get hurt. *–Cowboys at Raiders (11/19/95)*

On the Raiders not practicing on their soggy home field: I think when you play on a field like this, you have to *practice* on a field like this. You have to know this field better than your opponent. I remember Fred Biletnikoff. Every Saturday he would go down both sides and run all his patterns and make sure he had the right shoes, the right footing, and knew this field perfectly. *–Cowboys at Raiders (11/19/95)*

On a frozen day at Philadelphia's Veterans Stadium: The ball is not going to be easy to kick today because it's going to be hard. –*Cowboys at Eagles (12/10/95)*

On the Packers defense wilting under the Texas heat: You get a long Cowboys drive like that – a 14 or 15 play drive – and the Packers aren't going to have the conditioning to take a lot of those. You're up there in Green Bay where you've got like none degrees and you don't really fill your body with fluids. Then, with the wind chill, you get *below* none degrees, and so you don't drink a lot of fluids and you don't have anything to sweat. Now [Cowboys guard] Nate Newton has been here, it's been warm, so he drinks a lot of fluids and he has a lot of stuff to sweat out. Maybe the Green Bay guys don't have as much, and it will show on them if they have a lot of those [long] drives on their defense. –*NFC Championship Game, Packers at Cowboys (1/14/96)*

On the energy at Lambeau Field: Talk about a great scene. You just see and feel these fans and the excitement here. That's one of the big reasons Green Bay has played so well here; you can just *feel* this crowd. You can *feel* these people. You can feel the ghosts of greatness here. –*49ers at Packers (11/1/98)*

On what equals two feet: One elbow equals two feet. As does one *knee* equals two feet, which I learned many years ago. I remember we were doing a preseason game, and I thought a guy was out of bounds but his knee had touched down. Art McNally, who was the head of the officials, called and said because his knee was down you don't need two feet in, that one knee equals two feet. I never misunderstood that one again. –*NFC Wildcard, Packers at 49ers (1/3/99)*

On freezing days in the stands: They're always talking about the cold and how the players play in it. At least the players have benches and warm things down there, and they're out there running around. The fans just have to sit there and take it. Every time I see one of these cold weather games, I always marvel more at the fans than I do at the players. –*NFC Wildcard, Buccaneers at Eagles (12/31/00)*

On officials breaking up a scrum: It's always the umpire. The umpire is usually the biggest, strongest, toughest guy. It's always the umpire that, when there's a pile, he'll dive in on it. –*Super Bowl XL, Steelers vs. Seahawks (2/5/06)*

Chapter 11: STRATEGY & COACHING

49ers coach Bill Walsh reworks the battle plan with his quarterback.

On draw plays: I've always liked the draw, and I like it in that situation – on second-and-long. I *never* liked it on third-and-long because it was kind of a give-up play. *–Madden's first telecast, Saints at 49ers (9/23/79)*

On turnovers: You can have the greatest plans in the world – and players and ideas – but turnovers just seem to take so much out of you. Turnovers, and missed kicks. *–Packers at Buccaneers (10/21/79)*

On short practice weeks: I always liked to have a short week because it gave me an opportunity to complain. I would say, "It's unfair, we can't do it, we need sacrifice and dedication." But the players were much more attentive, and they seemed to have more concentration and work harder during a short week. And we always played better. *–Eagles at Cardinals (9/28/80)*

On Eagles defensive coordinator Marion Campbell's schemes: They have four [schemes]. They have a first-down defense. They have a nickel package, which is a passing-down defense. They have a short-yardage defense and they have a goal-line defense. All different people. And the thing he likes about it is that it keeps all the players interested…in the meetings, in the game, in practice, in *all* situations. *–Eagles at Cardinals (9/28/80)*

On "establishing the run": I never knew what that meant. And I never did like the term, probably because I didn't know what it meant. I always figured, if you establish something, then the *defense* establishes that and you can't do it. I think the best way to get a running game going is by passing – make the defensive line widen and the linebackers loosen. Then you can run the ball. – *Saints at Lions (10/12/80)*

On what makes a championship team: When you get to the fourth quarter and you're behind, you have to drive the ball down the field to win. That is what separates the average teams from the championship teams. – *Eagles at Seahawks (11/2/80)*

On the rise of the shotgun formation: That's something you don't see very often, but it may be a trend we're going to see – shotgun on first down. The ball was snapped to Jaworski, and he just handed it on a little delay to Wilbert Montgomery. What it did to the defense was bring defensive end Curtis McGriff up the field thinking it was a pass, and they ran right inside of him. –*Giants at Eagles (11/22/81)*

On Bengals' fourth-down call at the 49er goal line: You know what would be a pretty good play here? Fake the ball to [FB] Pete Johnson, keep it yourself and bootleg it into the endzone. I think that would get it. –*Super Bowl XVI, Bengals vs. 49ers (1/24/82)*

NOTE: Instead, the Bengals ran it with Johnson, who was hammered short of the goal line.

On second-and-long play calls: It's no fun to coach when it's second-and-22. There's no good play to think of in that situation. I used to always go to the sideline and take a drink of water. The quarterback is looking over, "What do you want, coach? What do you want?" And I'm over there taking a drink with my back to him. –*Rams at Raiders (12/18/82)*

On the decline of the straight-arm: MADDEN: That was a thing that was big in the old days. You used to always see the pictures of the running backs with their arms out, straight-arming you. You don't see those types of things anymore. The old straight-arm....

SUMMERALL: The old straight-arm was a lot more effective when the defenders didn't have any face masks.

MADDEN: That *would* make it effective. –*Rams at Raiders (12/18/82)*

On a meaningless third-down completion to Rob Carpenter: There's an example of why *Take what the defense gives you* doesn't make any sense. [QB] Scott Brunner had all those completions, but he didn't get a first down. You have to make something happen on offense. You can't just take what they give you. The defense gives you short to Carpenter, but it's not a first down so you have to kick a field goal. That saying should be out of football, *Take what* *the defense gives you.* Baloney! *Make* it happen. You gotta get first downs. You complete all those passes for one and two yards, but that won't get you in the endzone. –*Giants at Eagles (1/2/83)*

On trailing late in the fourth quarter: One of the things that could haunt the Rams is that they only have one time-out left. In a tight ball game, my God, that's like a missed extra point. –*Rams at Jets (9/25/83)*

On being at the goal line and trailing, with no times-out: I remember having this situation once with [QB] George Blanda. I said, "Let's run this 16-power blah-blah-blah." He said, "Okay, coach. But if you let me throw three slant passes to Warren Wells, I'll guarantee you a touchdown." I said, "You guarantee it? You got it." First one, incomplete. Second one, touchdown. We win the game. –*Rams at Jets (9/25/83)*

On the Cowboys having four consecutive comeback wins: That's one of those things you like to do when you *have* to, but you're not proud of having to do it week after week after week. –*Cowboys at Vikings (10/2/83)*

On losing streaks: Sometime when a team loses, they don't play very hard and don't play well. But sometimes when a team loses, they're trying *too* hard and they start to play scared and lose their confidence. –*Falcons at Jets (10/23/83)*

On the Redskins' famous Counter Trey play: They ran so much to the left last year that they put in a *new* play this year. It's called "Counter Trey." John Riggins will start to the left, and the [left] guard and [left] tackle will both pull. The defense holds, thinking he's gonna run to the left, but nope! Here he comes, right behind Grimm and Jacoby. That's a big play for them this year. They're making a living on that play. –*Redskins at Giants (11/13/83)*

On running the football: There's something about running that gives an offensive team confidence. Conversely, if you can't run, you *lose* your confidence. –*Giants at Redskins (12/17/83)*

On the sweep: I always felt the sweep was a poor short-yardage play. You have to run too far to get there. –*Cardinals at Giants (11/18/84)*

On the 1985 Bears defense: This defense is so good. I don't know if I've seen a defense this good since the [1970s] Pittsburgh Steelers, when they were dominant and winning those Super Bowls. They were probably the best defense that I had ever seen. I think this Bears defense ranks right up in that area. –*Bears at Cowboys (11/17/85)*

On 1985 Bears holding the Giants to 32 yards rushing: This Bear defense showed today that if you're going to have a chance against them, you'd better bring *more* than a running game. You'd better bring a little passing game, and with that passing game, you'd better bring a *lot* of pass protection. –*NFC Playoffs, Giants at Bears (1/5/86)*

On the Bears draining the clock with their running game: Coaches like Mike Ditka like to see running. They like to see it be successful, and they like to see it get first downs.... As a coach there's nothing more comfortable than to have a lead, to be at home in a playoff game and be able to run. Those are the three best feelings you can have. –*NFC Playoffs, Giants at Bears (1/5/86)*

On how much of his Raider offense was "hidden" during the preseason: I never hid *any* of it. We never had anything to hide. We kinda played where we flopped in there and rolled around and got dirty. Lotsa sweat and stuff. Then, throw a deep one every now and then. I just put it all in and played it. I never believed in that "hiding." –*Oilers at Cowboys (8/30/86)*

On poor tackling late in the season: It seems to me when teams get eliminated and they're not gonna be in it, that little level of intensity they lose is the tackling level. The championship teams still tackle well; the others don't. –*Giants at Redskins (12/7/86)*

On goal-line football: This is, to me, what football is all about – short yardage and goal line. In golf they say you drive for show and putt for dough. [In football] it's the same thing. You play in the middle of the field for show, and you do it down there for the dough. –*Giants at Steelers (9/5/87)*

On calling a draw play late in the game: A draw play is one of those plays that really doesn't work well at the end of a game.... A draw play works well when everyone's fresh and you go *Boom! Boom! Boom!* and run right by them. Late in the game, you get a defense that's kinda beaten down. They're tired. They're not going anywhere anyway. Then you run a draw and it's *Whap!* right into 'em. –*Eagles at Jets (12/20/87)*

On why so many teams adopted the Redskins' "Counter Trey": We see that run so much, where they pull off-guard and the off-tackle and the back takes a step and gets in there behind them. Now the 49ers are running it. The defense has to practice against it. And to practice against it, the offense has to learn it. So, you may as well use it. –*49ers at Saints (9/4/88)*

On being in the playoff hunt in late November: You don't go, at this point of the season, looking for a wildcard. You go for the whole thing. If you end up with the wildcard, you still got something; if you start *thinking* wildcard, then you usually end up empty-handed. *–Eagles at Cowboys (11/23/89)*

On whether to kick or receive to open a big game: Any time you get a big game, you *don't* want your offense out there first. *–Eagles at Giants (12/3/89)*

On Giants badly missing a long field goal into the wind: That's like *spitting* into the wind. You do that and you're gonna get wet a lot. *–Eagles at Giants (12/3/89)*

On 49ers getting an interception using the prevent defense: Everyone always says, "What does the prevent defense do except prevent you from winning?" But we just saw an example on that interception where a prevent defense *worked*. A prevent defense is like a well-officiated game. If the prevent defense works, it never gets mentioned the next day; if it doesn't work, that's all that gets talked about. *–49ers at Giants (9/6/92)*

On a defense's inability to stop the run: There's nothing that makes a defensive coach more mad than [an effective] running game. Everyone says *You have to stop the run, You have to stop the run*. When they run on you, it kills you. Because if you can't stop the run, they're going to do *everything* to you. All day. *–Eagles at Redskins (10/18/92)*

On the rise of the 1992 Cowboys: On this Cowboy team, there's a couple of ingredients that don't always go well together. They have the best record in the NFC, but they also have the youngest team. That's the thing that's always bothered their coaching staff. *Are we too young to handle all this success?* You always have to fight that, that they don't start thinking they're better than they are. *–Giants at Cowboys (11/26/92)*

On the Giants' offensive ineptitude: The Giants have twelve men on the field and have to take a timeout. The quarterback is looking right, looking left, and the ball gets snapped when he wasn't ready. They recover it, then they have to punt from the back line. When the wheels start to fall off, it's hard to keep the cart up. *–Giants at Cowboys (11/26/92)*

On tackling: Tackling is such a big part of this game. If you can't do that, then you can't play good defense. *–NFC Playoffs, Redskins at 49ers (1/9/93)*

On origin of the "tilted tackle" defensive formation: That alignment, where the nose tackle line up cockeyed, [Steelers DT] Joe Greene is the first guy that ever did that. We used to do some running inside on [Pittsburgh], then they started stacking him up in there and it would take two guys to block him. Then we couldn't block [LB] Jack Lambert. So, either Greene would beat a double-team, or Lambert would make the tackle. *And* we couldn't play-pass on Lambert anymore. So [the tilt formation] does take away a lot of things. – *Giants at Dolphins (12/5/93)*

On the time of possession statistic: Time of possession is good if, while you're possessing, you score points; if you possess and *don't* score points, it doesn't do you any good. –*Cowboys at Giants (1/2/94)*

On getting the first points on the board: In any game I was coaching, I always felt the toughest points were the *first* points. You always have to get something. I remember (during) my first year of coaching, George Blanda said, "Whatever it is, always take that field goal. Always get your points first. Once you get your points (on the board), the others come easier." George was the kicker, and he was ten years older than me. –*NFC Playoffs, Giants at 49ers (1/15/94)*

On Eagles coach Rich Kotite's play-calling strategy: He says, "There is no down or distance [chart]. If you get into a down or distance, then you become predictable. You get into a *rhythm*, then the defense gets in the same rhythm *with* you." So, he wants to stay out of a rhythm, to keep the *defense* out of a rhythm. –*Eagles at Cowboys (10/16/94)*

On Cowboys pulling Troy Aikman from the game after a violent hit to the chin: Anytime you hear "concussion" you have to take precaution, whether it's one on the chin, the head, whatever. They've got something in football over the years we haven't taken seriously enough. Concussion is a bruise to a brain, and I think it's a serious thing. If there's ever any doubt, the guy shouldn't play. The Cowboys are doing the right thing. –*Cowboys at Cardinals (10/23/94)*

On running the draw play on third-and-long: That's like wearing brown shoes and black socks. They're give-up plays. There's no good play for [third-and-28]. The draw is kind of a play you run just before you have to punt. When you don't care anymore, you just give up. You don't worry about how you look. Because you don't care. –*Cowboys at Giants (12/24/94)*

On play calling inside the 15-yard line: When you get down there and it's first down, you have to take *three* shots at the endzone. I learned that years and years ago from George Blanda. He said, "Look, the more shots you take at the endzone, the more chances you have at making touchdowns." That always made sense to me. –*49ers at Rams (10/22/95)*

On the wisdom of throwing downfield: When you throw passes over ten yards, all you have to do is complete one out of three. –*Cowboys at Raiders (11/19/95)*

On the Cowboys being stopped on fourth down, deep in their territory, late in the game: This is unbelievable! The score's tied! They're on the road! This is short-yardage defense! The Eagles are selling out against the run. They have everyone up. There's no chance to get that ball in there against that defense.... When you're in that area of the field, you *have* to punt the ball.... They deserve to lose. –*Cowboys at Eagles (12/10/95)*

On the downside of the West Coast Offense: Is there anything wrong with this West Coast Offense? To me, it's that they have to throw the ball too short and too often on third down. They complete passes then they have to punt. I think that's one of the ugliest sights in all of football – a completed third-down pass followed by a punt. –*NFC Wildcard, Eagles at 49ers (12/29/96)*

On throwing the ball in wintry Denver: I learned a lot about this bad weather the first time I came here as a head coach. George Blanda was my quarterback that day and it was snowing like this. I said, "Aww, this is terrible. We're not gonna be able to throw in this snow." George said, "No, snow is *great* weather to throw the ball in because you don't get a big pass rush. The defenders have a tough time because *they* slip and slide." He said, "If you can keep the footballs dry, this is the *best* weather to throw in." –*Panthers at Broncos (11/9/97)*

On the Bears offense throwing short passes and not attacking a rookie cornerback: You wonder why teams have success and then they go away from the success and go back to throwing short passes for none-yards. The Lions have a rookie playing corner out there in Kevin Abrams. They gave him some motion and Abrams broke a coverage and [the Bears] hit a big one to Ricky Proehl. You wonder why they don't go back to it. Why don't they say, "We've got a rookie corner playing over there; what are we throwing those none-yard passes for?" –*Bears at Lions (11/27/97)*

On the Panthers completing a third-down pass for no gain: Here's another one of those things that drives me crazy. I still don't understand this kind of football. You have third-and-three and you *have* to get the ball down the field. To come out on a bootleg and have a guy run a pattern for no yards – I really don't understand that. I don't know how that gets to be, where a guy can run that pattern short. When you complete a third-down pass then have to kick, that to me is dumb. –*Packers at Panthers (12/14/97)*

On offensive play-callers: One thing I know about guys who call plays – usually offensive coordinators who were ex-quarterbacks – once they start passing, they have a hard time getting back to the run. –*Packers at Panthers (12/14/97)*

On spending nights at the office: I never did that when I coached, and I never believed in that. I always said I may work real late and I may get up early, but I'm always gonna go home at night. –*Packers at Saints (12/14/97)*

On the Eagles calling a screen play without showing any downfield passing threat: They can't run that stuff yet. You run a screen when a team is afraid of your passing and they're backing off. The Eagles haven't thrown the ball successfully enough to run the screen or the draw.... Screen and draws are very hard to run when you haven't had any success in the passing game. –*Cowboys at Eagles (10/10/99)*

On stabilizing your offense early in the game: The way to get settled down is this – just let your offensive linemen tee-off on the defense, move those legs and run the ball right in behind them. If there's anything that settles an offense down, generally it's the running game. Specifically, the straight-ahead running game. –*NFC Wildcard, Cowboys at Vikings (1/9/00)*

On the Rams trailing the Buccaneers with 4:50 left to play: Somewhere between now and the end of the game, someone is gonna make a play that puts their team in the Super Bowl. –*NFC Championship Game, Buccaneers at Rams (1/23/2000)*

NOTE: As Madden was speaking these words, Kurt Warner was firing a 30-yard TD pass to Ricky Proehl and securing the NFC title for the Rams.

On the 2000 Rams turnover woes: They started having turnovers, and they started worrying *too much* about the turnovers. Then, the worry about the turnovers begot *more* turnovers.... Fumbling is something you don't think about. You don't say *We have to think about not fumbling*. When you think about *not* fumbling, then you're thinking about fumbling. You don't think about fumbling. You just go play. If you worry about fumbling, then you're just gonna look for a place to fall down. –*Vikings at Rams (12/10/00)*

On the Patriots' decision to attack offensively near the end of regulation, with the score tied: With no time outs, I think the Patriots, with this field position, have to run the clock out. You have to play for overtime now. I don't think you want to force anything here. You don't want to do anything stupid because you have no time outs and you're backed up.... I don't agree with what the Patriots are doing right here. I would play for overtime. –*Super Bowl XXXVI, Patriots vs. Rams, (2/3/02)*

NOTE: Tom Brady drove the Patriots 53 yards in the last minute to set up the game-winning field goal.

On the Patriots' Super Bowl-winning drive: What Tom Brady just did gives me goosebumps. –*Super Bowl XXXVI, Patriots vs. Rams (2/3/02)*

On divisional rivalries: I've always felt that when you get two divisional rivals playing each other, they know each other so well and it's a more conservative game. You will *not* do [risky] things, you *won't* open up. A lot of times you're playing against ghosts. *Four years ago, I tried to run that play and it got stuffed, or we fumbled it.* So, you tighten down. You play your most conservative games against your rivals. –*Giants at Eagles (10/28/02)*

On his most troublesome "ghosts," a.k.a. the Kansas City Chiefs: When I used to play ghosts, it was against Kansas City and their short-yardage and goal-line defense. I remember Buck Buchanan and Willie Lanier, and there was nothing we could do on them inside. I always worried about short-yardage and goal-line, and I'd remember what they did three and four years ago and say, "We can't do it." I used to say we couldn't score on the goal line against them. –*Giants at Eagles (10/28/02)*

On offensive success in the red zone: One of the things we were talking about with Bill Belichick last night was "red zone" offenses, inside the 20. Who's good, who's bad? He said, "Every team that is good in the red zone offensively can run the ball. If you can't run the ball, you're always gonna have trouble in this area." I totally agree with him. –*Patriots at Broncos (11/3/03)*

On a Colts' false-start penalty on 3rd-and-one: Those are the things that drive a coach crazy. You talk about discipline, and sometimes you think, *Oh, a guy's beard is too long* or something like that. That's not discipline. Discipline is when you get up there in short yardage and you play to the snap count. You're the home team. The crowd's not bothering you. There's no way you should jump. –*Vikings at Colts (11/8/04)*

On a bizarre Patriots defensive formation: I just saw the Patriots in a defense I have never seen before in my *life*. They had *no* defensive linemen. They just had linebackers and defensive backs in there. I've seen them use *one* defensive lineman, I think. I know I've seen them use *two* defensive linemen. On that play they had *zero* defensive linemen. The first time in the history of the National Football League. –*Patriots at Dolphins (12/20/04)*

On acquiring marginally-talented players: When you're signing a free agent or making a late-round draft choice and you're not sure of a guy, you always take either size or speed. That's the kind of thing Bill Parcells does and I've always believed in. You don't take a "tweener" in any one of those areas. You either take a big guy or a fast guy. –*Redskins at Cowboys (9/19/05)*

On Bill Parcells' offensive philosophy: On a Bill Parcells' team, second-and-ten is a running down…. The reason that Bill Parcells always runs on second-and-long is so he has a third-and-manageable. He doesn't want to throw an incomplete pass on second-and-long and then come up with third-and-long, where defenses can really throw all their blitzes at you. –*Redskins at Cowboys (9/19/05)*

On running the football: It's a lot easier to run the ball in the second half than it is in the first half; it's a lot easier to run it in the fourth quarter than the third quarter. And it's a heckuva lot easier to run it when you have a big lead in the fourth quarter, because for all intent and purposes, the defense is done. –*Chargers at Patriots (9/16/07)*

On what frightens defenses most: Defensive coaches are always afraid of speed. You ask what scares any defensive coach, any defensive guy, any defensive coordinator. More than anything, it's a wide receiver with speed. –*Chargers at Patriots (9/16/07)*

On taking a free kick after a fair catch: I was a head coach in the NFL for ten years, and I looked to use that play for ten years. I never did it. I always had it set up. *Okay, we're gonna do this. We'll take the fair catch and we'll get the free kick.* Never did. Saw it done once. Paul Brown did it once. –*AFC Wildcard, Colts at Chargers (1/3/09)*

Chapter 12: OTHER STUFF

Madden celebrates the Raiders' dethroning of Miami in the '74 playoffs.

On toughness: Toughness is someone doing something they don't enjoy doing, but they have to do it to be successful. *–Vikings at Packers (11/11/79)*

On the concept of a "team leader": There is a much-misunderstood thing about leadership in pro football. No one guy can be the leader of an *entire* team. At least, I've never seen one. In a group of 45 football players, there will usually be about five separate cliques. Maybe there's a married group with kids, a single group that parties a lot, the veterans, a group of second-line players or special teams guys. And you have to have a leader for every group. If you take a guy who has been playing awhile and is making really good money, lives in a great neighborhood, has a fine home and drives a big car...he's not going to be able to relate very well with some rookie from a small black school in the South who's just begun to escape poverty. *–Inside Sports, August 1980*

On coaches disliking road trips to the West Coast: Especially to southern California. They felt with the Hollywood influence and the movies, the players would get into that and it would be distracting. I don't know if they ever felt that way in northern California, at least not in Oakland. They used to not like to come there for a *different* reason. We used to have rats in the visiting locker room. They were going to exterminate them one day and I said, "Heck, no – Feed 'em!" Before the game I would tell the other coach,

"Don't worry. There are some rats in here. We're trying to get rid of them, but if you see one, don't worry." –*Packers at Rams (9/21/80)*

On the weak NFC Central Division: Someone's going to win that division, aren't they? Maybe the team that *loses the fewest games* will win that. I don't know that anyone is going to *win* it. People like the Eagles, they *win* the Eastern Division. People *win* divisions. Sometimes people just don't lose a division. One team *loses* more than the other. Does that make any sense? –*Eagles at Redskins (11/16/80)*

On NFL player size: You don't have to be that big. You have to be *good*. The only time they talk about someone being short is when they don't play well. –*Falcons at Eagles (12/7/80)*

On a camera shot of the evening moon over Tampa: I wonder if they'll ever play a football game up there. – *Bears at Buccaneers (12/20/80)*

On short-yardage defense: I always used to say that goal-line and short-yardage defense breeded fanaticism. –*NFC Wildcard, Rams at Cowboys (12/28/80)*

On "true" player weights of the '81 Rams: They have weight [goals] that they're given by the coaches, and sometimes they don't agree or like that weight. Fred Dryer used to wear weights underneath his shoulders so that he would weigh more when he got on the scale. He put weights underneath the t-shirt. Bill Bain, a backup guard, has a magnet that he can hold in his hand so, when he gets on the scale, he weighs 12 pounds less. They say the only guy that's constant is big [DT] Phil Murphy because he weighs 300 pounds and that's as high as the scale goes. When he gets on, they say, "Murphy – 300." As a coach I never worried about weight. I just worried about how they played. –*Packers at Rams (9/20/81)*

On staying warm during a frigid telecast at Shea Stadium: I went down to the locker room to see what the players were wearing, and they were showing me these pantyhose. They said they were the best thing you can wear. They gave us a package, so I took them out and put them on. –*Buccaneers at Jets (12/12/82)*

On a CBS *60 Minutes* promo: Someone told me during the [players] strike that one of the only good things about the strike is that everyone got to see *60 Minutes* in its entirety...at the scheduled time. –*Redskins at Giants (11/21/82)*

On a wild game at Shea Stadium: SUMMERALL: We've had 85-yard touchdown runs. We've had blocked field goals returned for a touchdown...two touchdown passes caught by Wesley Walker. We've had a fight....

MADDEN: *Brawls*. A fight is when *two* guys fight. When you get forty-nine guys on each side, you got ninety-eight guys and that's a brawl.

SUMMERALL: Yeah, I guess you're right.

MADDEN: *Two* guys fight; ninety-eight brawl. –*Rams at Jets (9/25/83)*

Recalling Tony Dorsett's 99-yard touchdown run against Vikings in 1982: He never got that football. He said he handed it to the referee. They left it in the game and they kicked the extra point. He said that ball is probably around some practice field today. –*Cowboys at Vikings (10/2/83)*

On a brawl between the Jets and Rams: MADDEN: Mark Gastineau's [fine] was the largest – a thousand dollars. Marty Lyons and Kenny Neil were each fined $750. The lowest fine was $300; [QB] Richard Todd got that. He said, "I was kinda proud of that."

SUMMERALL: There aren't too many fights where you get *both* quarterbacks involved...*and* fined.

MADDEN: That's what Todd said. He said, "I was out there looking for [Rams QB] Vince Ferragamo and couldn't find him. Then I looked for the kicker and couldn't find *him*. Then I walked back off. And it still cost me $300! –*Falcons at Rams (10/23/83)*

On the Cowboys' sluggish play in frozen Philadelphia: You know what I think the problem with the Cowboys today is? Most of them are wearing long underwear. The only guy that doesn't have it on is [DT] Randy White. But all the defensive backs have it. They got underwear, gloves, too much stuff on. They're not *playing*! I never did like that stuff. I kinda agree with [Vikings coach] Bud Grant. He didn't like it either. I think they get too concerned with staying warm. Randy White's got those bare arms playing out there. Go play like *that*. You don't need that [underwear] stuff. –*Cowboys at Eagles (11/6/83)*

On receiving an official team sweater from the Redskins: I've got to tell you an embarrassing story. I went to Washington and they were gonna give me a sweater. They said, "We've got double extra-large." I said, "No, no, I wear *triple* extra-large." They said, "No, this one is *big*. We gave one to [6-7, 300-lb] Dave Butz and it fits him." I said, "Well, if it's big enough for him, it's big enough for me." And the dag-gone thing *didn't fit*. Now that's embarrassing. –*Redskins at Giants (11/13/83)*

On Redskins QB Joe Theismann: I caught him before the game and he was wearing a rose in his coat. I said, "Gee, that's kinda funny, a football player coming to a game with a flower in his coat." He said, "Yeah, I don't know where they come from." Evidently before every game someone sends him a bunch of roses – on the road, at home, in the locker room. Maybe it's Bobby Beathard, the General Manager. Or [owner] Jack Kent Cooke. – *Redskins at Giants (11/13/83)*

On having any emotional involvement with the Raiders after retiring as their head coach: Not as much now. Had we done this game the first year I retired, it would have been a lot tougher. But there are only 15 players out of 49 that were there when I was there. You travel around and you get farther and farther away. It's really not that tough now. –*Giants at Raiders (11/27/83)*

On why linebacker Ted Hendricks' nickname was "Kick 'Em": When we first got Ted, we were having a practice, a dummy scrimmage. [RB] Marv Hubbard broke through the line. Ted was chasing him. He went to jump over him and he *didn't* jump over him. He kicked him in the head and knocked him out. So, when we found out Hubbard was okay, we started nicknaming him "Kick 'Em in the Head Ted." Then they shortened it to "Kick 'Em." That's his nickname now. –*Giants at Raiders (11/27/83)*

On a dull game at freezing Giants Stadium: I have a feeling, Pat, there's not a lot of emotion in this game. Doggonit, you can't play this game without emotion…. These teams are too calm. There's nothing going on here. You have to get excited about this thing to play it properly…. There's too many people walking around out here. Maybe you gotta get on 'em, yell at 'em on the sidelines or something. They're too *comfortable*. Throw the heaters out. *Who wants to play?!* –*Cardinals at Giants (12/4/83)*

After another player scuffle between the Bears and 49ers: You have those type of engagements in two parts of the game – one, *early* in a big game, when everyone is a little jittery and nervous; and two, *late* in a big game when one team is frustrated. –*NFC Championship Game, Bears at 49ers (1/6/85)*

On player holdouts during his tenure as Raiders coach: I didn't have that many. Most of the time that I coached they didn't get paid that much money. They didn't have that much to hold out for. I remember one year [DE] Ben Davidson was holding out for like 75 dollars. –*Eagles at Giants (9/8/85)*

On the strength of the Chicago and Dallas defenses: You know what I wish? You can't do it, it's a silly thing, but I wish these defenses could play *each other*. I'd like to see Ed "Too Tall" Jones go against Steve McMichael. I'd like to see a Dan Hampton go against a Randy White. See a Bill Bates run into a Gary Fencik. They don't do it that way, but these defenses are two tough-hombre defenses. –*Bears at Cowboys (11/17/85)*

On an apparent meaningless, late-season game for the '85 Bears: I think it means an awful *lot* to the Chicago Bears. I think the Bears are the best team in the NFL. I think they are going to go all the way and win the Super Bowl. If that's true, then they beat the Jets just because they're a better team. You don't need reasons to win. If you *do*, you're not going to go all the way. If you *need* reasons to win, then I don't think that they beat the Jets today, and I also don't think they go to and win the Super Bowl. –*Bears at Jets (12/14/85)*

On Bear-mania sweeping over Chicago: I have never seen a city support a football team – or be so excited about a football team – as I have being in Chicago this week. –*NFC Championship Game, Rams at Bears (1/12/86)*

On the rise of the New York Giants: Last year I thought the Bears had the best defense that I'd ever seen. This year, in the last two games – last week against the 49ers and today against the Redskins – I feel that the Giants are as good a defense that's played in this league. –*NFC Championship Game, Redskins at Giants (1/11/87)*

On the outcome of the Super Bowl: The gap between winning and losing the Super Bowl is the biggest gap there is in sports. The winner is the world champion; the loser gets thrown back with the other twenty-six. –*Super Bowl XXI, Giants vs. Broncos (1/25/87)*

On winning the Super Bowl: It's one of those things that is big when it happens and gets bigger as the years go on.... I'll tell ya, this is as good as it gets. It doesn't get any better than this. And the great thing about it, it lasts *forever*. It's not something that's not there tomorrow. –*Super Bowl XXI, Giants vs. Broncos (1/25/87)*

On computers playing a larger role in football: Everyone takes [information from] the game and puts it in a computer, and they'll say, "On every first down, they'll do this." Then *your* computer says, "You did *this* every first down." Then you come up with *Don't do it every first down*. And that's what they're doing, if that makes any sense. So much for computers. You still need guys. –*Cowboys at 49ers (8/22/87)*

On the defending champion Giants starting 0-2 and their strike team going winless: The Giants, whether they're [on strike or not], just have to be sick about this, starting off 0-3 and [about to go 0-4]. I don't know that they're not digging a hole that's going to be impossible to get out of.... Before they went out on strike, they weren't playing all that well. They're 0-3 now but you have to remember they got the "0-2" themselves. –*Redskins at Giants (10/11/87)*

NOTE: At the end of the '87 strike, the Giants had a 0-5 record; they would finish 6-9 and miss the playoffs.

On an ugly performance by the Giants strike team in front of 9,123 fans: If I were the Giants, down 31-12 with six minutes left, I'd just run the clock out then go in and hope for some kind of [labor] settlement. –*Redskins at Giants (10/11/87)*

On a strike game with replacement players, and the Saints about to score: I'm wondering right now what the regular Bears and the regular Saints are thinking. They say these games are gonna count. I think they have a lawsuit up between the National Labor Relations Board regarding this game. But what are [the real players] doing right now? Are they rooting for the Saints to get in the endzone? Or for the Bears to stop them? Or what? Or do they *care*? I don't know. –*Saints at Bears (10/18/87)*

On how players react to injuries: I've always found that when a guy keeps his helmet on and keeps it strapped up, he's usually okay. When a guy is really hurt, it seems the first thing that comes off is that chinstrap; the second thing is the hat itself.... Just an observation over the years. –*Giants at Redskins (10/2/88)*

On a trio of Rams fans wearing watermelons on their heads: I don't know if they're real or not, but they sure look stupid. How can a guy get dressed like that to go to a game? What do you say? "I think I'll put on my watermelon head and sunglasses and go to the game and look stupid?" –*49ers at Rams (10/16/88)*

On a tense fourth quarter at RFK Stadium: This is what football is all about! This is everyone giving everything they've got. Guys cracking, the emotion, the night, the dirt, the grass, the linebackers, big old arms, mud on the thing, stuff hanging out, fourth quarter, tired, sweat. This is what it's all about! –*Saints at Redskins (11/6/88)*

On a bizarrely dressed couple at Candlestick Park: Those two have no idea whether you blow [the ball] up or stuff it. They were looking for a party and ended up at a game. –*NFC Playoffs, Vikings at 49ers (1/1/89)*

On new Cowboys owner Jerry Jones celebrating on the sideline after his first preseason win: If I had one suggestion for owners, it would be *Don't go down on the sideline during a game when your team wins*. Because if you do that, they're gonna expect you to be there when you lose, too. And that's not fun. –*Cowboys at Chargers (8/13/89)*

On football mothers: The one that knows more about a player than anyone is their mother. Because she's the one that, no matter what happens in the game, watches her son on every play. When the mother says, "You played well," you played well. When the mother says, "You didn't play well," that guy didn't play well. They don't watch anything else. That's all she cares about. –*Eagles at Cowboys (11/23/89)*

On a shot of the Fuji blimp over RFK Stadium: What do blimps do when there's no game to go to? What else do they do? They don't do any good, but they still make them.... I'd never want to go up in one of those things. Everyone says, "I'd like to go up in one of those." Not me. –*Eagles at Redskins (10/21/90)*

On the custom-fitted jerseys of the Eagles defensive line: I was talking to Reggie White one time. He was saying that they wanted the jerseys tight on top, so that [offensive linemen] couldn't hold. What the guy did was make the jerseys tight *all the way*. He said it made them all look too fat. So, this year they have a design where they're tight up on top, and they give them some looseness in the body for the combilations. –*Packers at Eagles (12/16/90)*

On the Chiefs' mascot Warpaint, a stallion that circled the field after every Kansas City score: I remember playing here when I was coaching the Oakland Raiders. They had that horse here called Warpaint. One time they scored 42 points against us, and we darned near killed Warpaint. That last time [KC scored] his tongue was halfway down to the ground. I told my guys after the game, "Hey, you guys darned-near killed Warpaint today." From then on, I'd always say, "Let's just keep Warpaint in the corral. We almost killed Warpaint once. I don't want him running around that field anymore." –*Redskins at Chiefs (11/15/92)*

On the Chiefs' fast 28-0 lead: Warpaint is lucky he's out there on that ranch. –*Redskins at Chiefs (11/15/92)*

On CBS's odd Thanksgiving turkey: MADDEN: A six-legged turkey, man. That's something.

SUMMERALL: The only thing I can tell you is he was very hard to catch.

MADDEN: Well, yeah. You got *this* leg with the back power, *this* leg with the middle power, *this* leg with the front power, then you have both sides going.

SUMMERALL: You should see him jump.

MADDEN: We go down the highway [in the Madden Cruiser] and that's like an 18-wheel turkey. We can give legs to everybody...to linemen and linebackers and nose tackles. *–Giants at Cowboys (11/26/92)*

On teams easily running the ball on the Chicago Bears: This is one of the reasons that the Bears aren't as good as they used to be. It's because they don't have that dominant defense anymore. Remember when they were a great team? You couldn't *do* this. You couldn't *block* like this. You couldn't get *holes* like this. You wouldn't have *running lanes* like this.... They lost a lot of great players on defense, and they didn't replace them with great players. *–Bears at Cowboys (12/27/92)*

On gauging a player's speed: I used to be able to tell how fast a guy was by how far the mud went up the back of his pants. If the mud just went a little way up when he would run, the guy was slow. A guy like Cliff Branch, when he would run, would kick mud all the way up to his shoulder pads. Art Shell would kick it up to the top of his socks. *–NFC Championship Game, Cowboys at 49ers (1/17/93)*

On Vikings QB Jim McMahon suffering another head injury: I think if a guy has had a concussion, he shouldn't play anymore. I don't agree with [putting him back in the game]. They always talk about boxing, and boxing being archaic, but if a boxer gets knocked out he can't fight for another month. Sometimes in football we say, "Oh, a guy has a slight concussion; he'll be right back in." I don't know if I ever agreed with that. *–NFC Wildcard, Vikings at Giants (1/9/94)*

On a camera shot of a jet skier in San Leandro Bay: That looks like fun, but you've gotta be at the ball game. How can you do that stuff when there's ball being played? What kind of guy says, "Well, the Cowboys are in town, the Raiders are back [in Oakland], the Cowboys and the Raiders – I think I'll go jet skiing?" What kind of guy is that? *–Cowboys at Raiders (11/19/95)*

On Eagles FB Kevin Turner returning to the game after a concussion: They said earlier that he had a concussion. Now he's back in there. Either he didn't have a concussion or he's *playing* with a concussion. They had a lot of medical people down there looking at him. I saw them. That's the thing that you wonder about sometimes. Last week Steve Young of the 49ers gets a concussion. They take him out. They bring in the backup, Jeff

Brohm. Jeff Brohm gets hurt and they bring Steve Young back in. Either Steve Young had a concussion and shouldn't have been playing and can't go back in, or he should have been *in there*. Sometimes teams do things in the heat of battle that, when you kinda analyze it after, don't make a heckuva lot of sense. –*Packers at Eagles (9/7/97)*

NOTE: In 2016, Turner died from CTE at age 46.

On concussions: I'm a firm believer that they have to study concussions more in this league, and keep better records than they do, and have an objective program for concussions rather than just whatever the guy says he feels. –*Cowboys at 49ers (11/2/97)*

On a camera shot of the Green Bay night: Can you believe a cow jumped over the moon? –*49ers at Packers (11/1/98)*

On the tense ending to the 1998 NFC Championship: I don't know that I've done a game in the broadcast booth where my palms were sweaty. They are now. –*NFC Championship Game, Falcons at Vikings (1/17/99)*

On Eagles guard John Welbourn: MADDEN: He went to the University of California and majored in Rhetoric. Now what in the heck is a major in Rhetoric?

SUMMERALL: Do you know what rhetoric is?

MADDEN: I think it's what you do when you talk a lot. Like someone says, "That guy's full of rhetoric. All he does is talk rhetoric." It's talking, I think. –*Eagles at Cowboys (9/3/00)*

On Eagles defensive end Hugh Douglas: You know what I like about Hugh Douglas? He keeps candy in his locker. He's a big candy guy. Anyone can come to his locker and take candy as long as they put the bowl back. He has a big pumpkin full of candy. One time they didn't put it back so he just threw all the candy away. He said, "Sometimes you just have to teach 'em a lesson. Sometimes you have to kill a fly with a sledgehammer." He said now they're being good; he has all the candy back at his locker. –*NFC Wildcard, Buccaneers at Eagles (12/31/00)*

On football's physical toll: If you play one down of regular season football in the National Football League, your body will never be normal the rest of your life. –*Rams at Eagles (9/9/01)*

On the Lions' first-year GM Matt Millen: Matt Millen has been brought here to turn this thing around. We've known Matt Millen for a long time and respect him as much as anyone. He's going to [turn the franchise around].

He's the right guy for the job and he's going to get it done. But I'll tell you this: It's a big, big job. –*Packers at Lions (11/22/01)*

NOTE: During Millen's tenure as Detroit GM (2001-08), the Lions went 31-84. He was fired three games into the '08 season. The team finished 0-16.

On his final broadcast with Pat Summerall: As we start the fourth quarter, Pat, it's our last fourth quarter together. I just wanna say thanks for a lot of memories of a lot of great quarters. 21 years. You multiply all those years by all those games, and you multiply that by all those quarters, it's been very, very special. And *you* made it very special. –*Super Bowl XXXVI, Rams vs. Patriots (2/3/02)*

On his favorite NFL season: I thought the most fun in the National Football League – and I've been saying this for years – was 1985 and the 1985 Bears. I thought *that* was the most fun in football since I've been in this business. –*Packers at Bears (10/7/02)*

On toy train sets: Did you ever get a train as a kid? I think everyone did. At some point as a kid you always wanted a train. And at some point, you always got a train. And usually, like two weeks after, it didn't work anymore. Broken. I don't know anyone that ever got a train and stayed with it for years. –*Steelers at Buccaneers (12/23/02)*

On a woeful offensive showing by the Buccaneers: This Tampa Bay offense is having trouble just getting back to the line of scrimmage. Remember Monte Clark, the old offensive line coach for years at Miami and then the head coach at Detroit? When you'd say, "How ya doing, Monte?" he'd say, "Just trying to get back to the line of scrimmage." That's what the Buccaneers are doing: Just trying to get back to the original line of scrimmage. –*Steelers at Buccaneers (12/23/02)*

On the listless Super Bowl performance by the Raiders: The Raider defense looks like they're lethargic and slow. This is the Super Bowl! This is the world championship! This is *it*! You have the feeling that the Buccaneers are out there fighting for a world championship. I don't know that I have that same feeling about the Raiders.... Whatever that thing is that you have to come up with to change momentum, to make a play, to get something to happen, the Raiders don't look like they're worried about that! That's the way I feel. Just looking at the sideline and the guys on the field, there isn't [any fire]. This thing is emotional! This is for the championship of the world! This is Super Bowl 37 we're talking about here! *Tampa Bay* understands it. –*Super Bowl XXXVII, Buccaneers vs. Raiders (1/26/03)*

To co-host Al Michaels, on the Colts' shocking 21-point comeback: I think this is very, very close to "Do you believe in miracles?" I think we're getting close. I'm not saying we're there, but *this* is amazing! –*Colts at Buccaneers (10/6/03)*

On Buccaneers WR Keyshawn Johnson being de-activated due to breaking team rules: My feeling is, the things you allow to happen when you *win*, you have to live with when you *lose*. That replay we just had of Keyshawn arguing back and forth with [coach] John Gruden? That was a year ago. I think if you let that stuff go when you win, then when you start to lose it becomes a cancer.... You get to the point where you get pushed so far as a person, as a coach, then you have to get rid of it. –*Giants at Buccaneers (11/24/03)*

On Packers QB Brett Favre playing on the day after his father's death: I have no idea how Brett Favre is going to do it. Yesterday when we talked to him, he had so much spirit and energy. He felt so good about his team, about what they were doing and what they were going to do. Then a couple hours later he hears his father dies. There's no road map for this. There's nothing that says this is the *right* way you handle it, and this is the *wrong* way you handle it, or *this* is how you do it. This is something that has to shock you. How Brett Favre is going to be able to handle this, I have no idea. –*Packers at Raiders (12/22/03)*

On Brett Favre continuing to play during a blowout victory, the day after his father died: He made a commitment that he was going to play in this game, and I think [the Packers] made a commitment to him. That this is *his* game. The worst thing they can do is take it away from him now. This is going to be a long night for him. After this game is over, it's going to be very difficult for Brett Favre. I don't think you want to speed that up. –*Packers at Raiders (12/22/03)*

On Carolina Panthers owner Jerry Richardson, a former NFL wide receiver: I played in an All-Star game with him. He and I roomed together. When I first met him, he said, "I'm from Wuffa College." I said, "What? There's no college named Wuffa! That's not even a *word*." I couldn't understand him.... It was "*Wofford* College." –*NFC Wildcard, Cowboys at Panthers (1/3/04)*

On the NFL's overuse of instant replay on fumbles: Let's get back to where a fumble is a fumble. If someone has the ball and they get hit and they fumble it, it's a doggone fumble. Now, every time there's a fumble, we have to look, *Is the elbow down? Is the knee down? Is the foot?* All those types of things, instead of it just being a fumble. –*Colts at Patriots (9/9/04)*

On certain players having prescience: I used to have a player like that – Gene Upshaw. No matter what happened, after the game he would say he had a dream about it. *He dreamt that we beat 'em by three touchdowns. He dreamt that Stabler threw four touchdown passes.* I said, "Hey look, when you have those dreams, if you know what's gonna happen before, tell me! Tell me what's gonna happen!" –*Vikings at Packers (11/21/05)*

The All-Time All-Madden Team
(Based on career nominations)

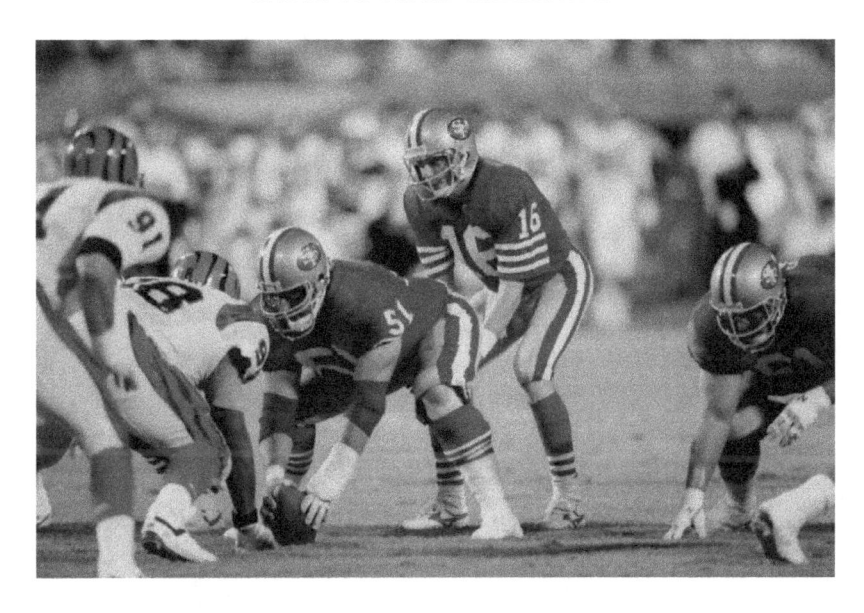

Quarterback – Joe Montana
Running Backs – Emmitt Smith, Barry Sanders
Guards – Nate Newton, Randall McDaniel
Tackles – Jackie Slater, Larry Allen
Tight End – Keith Jackson
Wide Receivers – Jerry Rice, Gary Clark
Defensive ends – Richard Dent, Charles Haley
Defensive tackles – Reggie White, Dan Hampton
Linebackers – Lawrence Taylor, Mike Singletary, Rickey Jackson
Cornerbacks – Darrell Green, Deion Sanders
Safeties – Ronnie Lott, Darren Woodson
Special Teams – Bill Bates, Reyna Thompson
Returner – Dave Meggett
Kicker – Kevin Butler

A

Aaron Taylor, 66
Al Vermeil, 64
Amp Lee, 39
Andre Waters, 78
Anthony Miller, 49
Archie Manning, 8
Art McNally, 94
Arthur Cox, 46

B

Barry Sanders, 22, 36, 38, 39, 40, 117
Ben Roethlisberger, 24
Bernard Williams, 66
Bill Bates, 75, 76, 83, 87, 109, 117
Bill Belichick, 7, 42, 50, 103
Bill Bergey, 68
Bill Fralic, 54
Bill Parcells, 2, 3, 4, 29, 32, 47, 61, 69, 70, 76, 83, 91, 103, 104
Bill Walsh, 5, 20, 23, 69, 95
Billy Martin, 64
Bob Griese, 18, 48
Bob Holly, 11
Bobby Beathard, 108
Bobby Humphrey, 46
Bobby Johnson, 46
Bobby Lane, 15
Boomer Esiason, 15
Brad Benson, 71
Brent Fullwood, 33
Brett Favre, 19, 21, 22, 24, 115
Brian Sipe, 9
Broderick Sargent, 35
Bruce Collie, 54
Bruce Harper, 29
Bubba Paris, 55
Buck Buchanan, 103
Bud Carson, 6
Bud Grant, 107
Buddy Ryan, 4, 5
Butch Johnson, 44, 45

C

Cap Boso, 48
Carl Banks, 71, 85
Carlton Bailey, 38
Cecil Sapp, 88
Charles Haley, 65, 66, 117
Charles Mann, 62, 64
Charlie Trippi, 22
Chet Brooks, 76
Chris Canty, 67
Chris Vallerial, 59
Chuck Cecil, 77
Chuck Noll, 3
Claudie Minor, 51
Cliff Branch, 45, 47, 112
Clinton Portis, 42
Clyde Simmons, 63
Cookie Gilchrist, 34
Craig Morton, 8
Curtis Martin, 40
Curtis McGriff, 96

D

Dalton Hilliard, 36
Dan Hampton, 61, 109, 117
Dan Marino, 16, 20, 21, 22
Dan Reeves, 20
Danny White, 11, 61, 82
Darrell Green, 73, 74, 77, 78, 117
Darren Woodson, 117
Darrin Nelson, 34
Daryl Grant, 61
Daryl Johnston, 38
Dave Butz, 60, 61, 62, 107
Dave Campo, 6
Dave Casper, 46
Dave Krieg, 18, 19
Dave Levy, 18
Dave Logan, 61
Dave Meggett, 39, 117
Dave Smigelsky, 82
David Archer, 13
Deion Sanders, 48, 78, 117
Dennis Harrison, 60
Denny Green, 23
Derek Kennard, 57
Derrick Thomas, 72
Desmond Howard, 55
Dick LeBeau, 79
Dick Vermeil, 1, 2, 6
Don Coryell, 2
Doug Cosbie, 70
Doug Plank, 76
Doug Williams, 17
Drew Bledsoe, 21
Dwight Freeney, 66

E

Earl Campbell, 27
Ed "Too Tall" Jones, 52, 109
Eddie DiBartolo, 5

Edgerrin James, 42
Elvis Patterson, 83
Emmitt Smith, 21, 36, 37, 39, 42, 57, 117
Emmitt Thomas, 75
Eric Allen, 76
Eric Dickerson, 29, 91
Eric Gamble, 3
Erik Williams, 56, 57, 58
Ernest Byner, 64
Ernest Gray, 44
Ernest Jackson, 14
Everson Walls, 73, 75

F

Fred Barnett, 48
Fred Biletnikoff, 45, 93
Fred Dryer, 106
Fred Hoaglin, 62
Freddie Solomon, 12

G

Gary Clark, 117
Gary Fencik, 75, 109
Gary Hogeboom, 10, 12
Gary Reasons, 84
George Adams, 31, 34
George Blanda, 97, 100, 101
George Halas, 1
George Rogers, 53
Gerry Ellis, 27
Greg Bell, 34, 35
Greg Coleman, 82
Greg Manusky, 71, 85

H

Harold Carmichael, 43, 44
Harry Carson, 69
Harvey Martin, 60
Henry Lawrence, 52
Herschel Walker, 32
Hines Ward, 24
Howard Cross, 48
Hugh Douglas, 113
Hugh McIlhenny, 86

I

Ironhead Heyward, 38

J

Jack Kent Cooke, 108

Jack Lambert, 100
Jack Reynolds, 69
Jackie Slater, 117
Jake Plummer, 22
James Brown, 66
James Hodgins, 41
James Lofton, 44
Jan Stenerud, 81
Jay Hilgenberg, 51, 53
Jay Schroeder, 13, 14, 17
Jeff Brohm, 113
Jeff Fuller, 76
Jeff Garcia, 23
Jeff George, 20
Jeff Hostetler, 17, 18
Jeff Rodenberger, 33
Jeff Zimmerman, 55
Jerome Bettis, 38
Jerome Brown, 54, 63
Jerry Ball, 55
Jerry Burns, 4
Jerry Eckwood, 25
Jerry Gray, 76
Jerry Jones, 111
Jerry Rice, 43, 48, 117
Jerry Richardson, 115
Jim Burt, 61, 63, 82
Jim Everett, 16
Jim Harbaugh, 18
Jim McMahon, 12, 13, 20, 21, 112
Jim Mora, 33
Jim Otto, 68
Jim Plunkett, 10
Jimbo Covert, 53
Jimmy Johnson, 5, 63, 86, 93
Joe Cain, 39
Joe Gibbs, 2, 4, 11, 17, 31, 61, 70, 73, 78
Joe Greene, 99
Joe Jacoby, 52, 55, 56, 64
Joe Klecko, 62
Joe McLaughlin, 82
Joe Montana, 12, 14, 15, 16, 17, 23, 90, 117
Joe Morris, 33, 34
Joe Namath, 15
Joe Theismann, 10, 17, 108
Joe Walton, 10
John Brodie, 11
John Bunting, 69
John Elway, 13, 15, 19, 62
John Fourcade, 14, 15
John Gruden, 115
John Jefferson, 44
John Marshall, 24, 63
John McKay, 1
John Riggins, 28, 30, 31

John Robinson, 2, 3, 25, 29, 34
John Stallworth, 14, 47
John Taylor, 48
John Welbourn, 113
John Wojciechowski, 54
Johnny Grier, 92
Johnny Johnson, 75
Jon Runyan, 59
Jumbo Elliott, 55
Jumpy Geathers, 66

K

Keith Byars, 78
Keith Griffin, 31, 91
Keith Jackson, 5, 117
Kelly Goodburn, 86
Ken Clarke, 18
Ken Reaves, 53
Ken Stabler, 10, 11
Kenny Hill, 91
Kenny Neil, 107
Kenny Stabler, 13, 14, 15
Kerry Collins, 23
Kevin Abrams, 101
Kevin Butler, 83, 92, 117
Kevin Gogan, 56, 58
Kevin Turner, 112
Keyshawn Johnson, 115
Kurt Gouveia, 72
Kurt Warner, 22, 23

L

Larry Allen, 58, 117
Larry Csonka, 23
Lawrence Taylor, 14, 63, 68, 69, 70, 71, 72, 117
Lee Roy Selmon, 61
Lee Woodall, 40
Leon Lett, 67
Leroy Hoard, 41
Leroy Irvin, 76
Lin Elliott, 86
Lionel Manual, 47
Lionel Manuel, 47
Lomas Brown, 65
Louie Kelcher, 60
Louis Giammona, 69
Louis Lipps, 14
Louis Wright, 75
Lyle Alzado, 52
Lynn Cain, 25

M

Marcus Allen, 30
Marion Campbell, 95
Mark Bavaro, 19, 46, 47
Mark Bortz, 52
Mark Collins, 78
Mark Gastineau, 107
Mark Lee, 77
Mark Malone, 14
Mark Moseley, 83
Mark Rypien, 17, 18
Mark Tuinei, 56, 58
Mark van Eeghen, 28, 35
Marshall Faulk, 22, 41, 42
Martin Gramática, 88
Marty Lyons, 107
Marv Hubbard, 35, 108
Matt Bahr, 86
Matt Elliott, 55
Matt Millen, 69, 71, 113
Maurice Carthon, 34
Maury Buford, 84
Max Runager, 83
Mel Blount, 75
Michael Carter, 62
Michael Haddix, 36
Michael Irvin, 49, 57
Mick Luckhurst, 82
Mike Augustyniak, 28
Mike Barber, 44
Mike Busch, 14
Mike Ditka, 2, 4, 6, 12, 15, 33, 52, 98
Mike Golic, 64
Mike Guman, 28
Mike Holmgren, 6, 19, 41
Mike Kenn, 57
Mike Pitts, 63
Mike Singletary, 37, 72, 117
Mike Tomczak, 17
Monte Clark, 114
Morten Anderson, 84, 86

N

Nate Newton, 36, 53, 54, 56, 57, 64, 94, 117
Nick Buoniconti, 72
Norm Van Brocklin, 9, 15

O

Odessa Turner, 85
Olin Kreutz, 59
Ottis Anderson, 26, 31, 32, 90

P

Pat Swilling, 38
Paul Brown, 1, 104
Paul Warfield, 48
Pete Banaszak, 25, 35
Pete Johnson, 96
Peyton Manning, 24
Phil Murphy, 106
Phil Pozderac, 52
Phil Simms, 9, 16, 19, 20, 46
Pierce Holt, 63

R

Randall Cunningham, 5, 17, 19, 49
Randall McDaniel, 117
Randy Moss, 49, 50
Randy White, 52, 107, 109
Randy Wright, 13
Rashaan Salaam, 40
Raul Allegre, 33, 84
Ray Guy, 81, 86, 87
Ray Perkins, 9, 28
Raymont Harris, 39
Reggie Roby, 87
Reggie White, 60, 63, 64, 111, 117
Renaldo Nehemiah, 12, 44
Reyna Thompson, 85, 117
Rich Kotite, 100
Rich Milot, 69
Richard Dent, 63, 64, 65, 117
Richard Todd, 10, 107
Rickey Jackson, 5, 117
Ricky Watters, 37, 38, 39
Rob Carpenter, 28, 96
Robert Goff, 65
Rodney Hampton, 39
Roger Craig, 32, 34, 35, 36
Roger Ruzek, 85
Roger Staubach, 12, 20
Ron Ferrari, 69
Ron Jaworski, 8, 9
Ronnie Lott, 36, 74, 76, 77, 117
Roy Green, 46
Russ Francis, 12
Russ Grimm, 52

S

Sam Mills, 71
Scott Brunner, 9, 60, 96
Sean Farrell, 82, 83
Sean Landeta, 83, 84
Sean Payton, 15
Shannon Sharpe, 49
Sid Luckman, 21
Slobodan Živojinović, 47
Stacy Toran, 47
Stan Humphries, 17
Stan Walters, 69
Steve Bartkowski, 10, 11
Steve Bradley, 15
Steve Courson, 53
Steve Cox, 85
Steve DeBerg, 12, 15, 20
Steve McNair, 23
Steve Rehage, 76
Steve Young, 6, 15, 65, 112

T

Ted Hendricks, 69, 108
Terrell Davis, 41
Terry Metcalf, 26
Timmy Newsome, 29, 45
Todd Christensen, 10
Tom Brady, 23, 24, 102, 103
Tom Brown, 35
Tom Flores, 3
Tom Holmoe, 76
Tom Jackson, 70
Tom Landry, 1, 2, 20, 29, 52, 73, 91
Tom Rathman, 35, 37, 71
Tom Waddle, 48, 86
Tony Dorsett, 2, 25, 27, 28, 29, 32, 107
Tony Dungy, 23, 40
Tony Franklin, 80, 81, 82
Tony Galbreath, 32
Tony Hill, 44
Torin Smith, 62
Travis Jervey, 41
Trent Green, 22
Troy Aikman, 17, 18, 21, 49, 56, 57, 58, 64, 77, 100
Troy Benson, 71
Troy Polamalu, 79
Ty Law, 41

V

Vaughn Hebron, 38
Vernon Dean, 74
Vince Ferragamo, 107
Vince Lombardi, 6, 35
Vinnie Testaverde, 15
Vyto Kab, 45, 46

W

Walter Payton, 26, 30, 31, 33, 74, 75
Warren Bryant, 51
Warren Moon, 21
Warren Sapp, 66
Warren Wells, 97
Warrick Dunn, 40, 41
Wayne Smith, 74
Weeb Ewbank, 3, 4
Wes Chandler, 43
Wes Hopkins, 31, 78
Wilbert Montgomery, 26, 27

William "Refrigerator" Perry, 61, 62
William Fuller, 57
Willie Broughton, 63
Willie Lanier, 103
Willie Moscone, 85
Willie Roaf, 57

Z

Zeke Mowatt, 84
Zendejas Brothers, 85

Photo/Art Credits

Madden & Summerall: Courtesy CBS Incorporated

Page 25: Courtesy ABC Visual Communication

Page 68, 73: ©Getty Images

All other photos: Danyluk private collection

Cover art: Zack Wallenfang

Cover design: Sam Wall

Edited by: Bill Mula, ex-Hoogovens Heroes

About the Author

Tom Danyluk is a freelance writer who has been covering the NFL since 1987. He joined Pro Football Weekly in 2004, where he was a feature columnist through 2013. He has won several Pro Football Writers Association awards, including the coveted "Best Column" honor in 2009.

His first book, *The Super '70s*, was went to print in 2005. *The Lost Super Bowls*, a fictional history of the early AFL, was published in July of 2016. *None Yards!* is his latest effort. Tom currently lives in Chicago with his wife Andleeb.

Ω

CPSIA information can be obtained
at www.ICGtesting.com
Printed in the USA
BVHW010243110122
625974BV00016B/218